D1602681

LIBRARY OF PHILOSOPHY AND RELIGION

General Editor: John Hick
Danforth Professor, Claremont Graduate School,
Claremont, California

This series of books explores contemporary religious under-
standings of humanity and the universe. The books contri-
bute to various aspects of the continuing dialogues between
religion and philosophy, between scepticism and faith, and
between the different religions and ideologies. The authors
represent a correspondingly wide range of viewpoints. Some
of the books in the series are written for the general
educated public and others for a more specialized philosophical or theological readership.

Selected titles

H. A. Hodges	GOD BEYOND KNOWLEDGE
Christopher Ives	ZEN AWAKENING AND SOCIETY
J. Kellenberger	THE COGNITIVITY OF RELIGION
	GOD RELATIONSHIPS WITH AND WITHOUT GOD
Jonathan L. Kvanvig	THE POSSIBILITY OF AN ALL-KNOWING GOD
Hywel D. Lewis	PERSONS AND LIFE AFTER DEATH
Julius L. Lipner	THE FACE OF TRUTH
Eric Lott	VEDANTIC APPROACHES TO GOD
Geddes MacGregor	REINCARNATION AS A CHRISTIAN HOPE
Hugo A. Meynell	AN INTRODUCTION TO THE PHILOSOPHY OF BERNARD LONERGAN
F. C. T. Moore	THE PSYCHOLOGICAL BASIS OF MORALITY
Dennis Nineham	THE USE AND ABUSE OF THE BIBLE
Martin Prozesky	RELIGION AND ULTIMATE WELL-BEING
D. Z. Phillips	BELIEF, CHANGE AND FORMS OF LIFE
Bernard M. G. Reardon	HEGEL'S PHILOSOPHY OF RELIGION
	KANT AS PHILOSOPHICAL THEOLOGIAN
Bruce R. Reichenbach	THE LAW OF KARMA: A PHILOSOPHICAL STUDY
Joseph Runzo	REASON, RELATIVISM AND GOD
Arvind Sharma	A HINDU PERSPECTIVE ON THE PHILOSOPHY OF RELIGION
Patrick Sherry	RELIGION, TRUTH AND LANGUAGE GAMES
	SPIRIT, SAINTS AND IMMORTALITY
Ninian Smart	CONCEPT AND EMPATHY
	RELIGION AND THE WESTERN MIND
Wilfred Cantwell Smith	TOWARDS A WORLD THEOLOGY
Norman Solomon	JUDAISM AND WORLD RELIGION
Jonathan Sutton	THE RELIGIOUS PHILOSOPHY OF VLADIMIR SOLOVYOV
Linda J. Tessier (editor)	CONCEPTS OF THE ULTIMATE
Shivesh Chandra Thakur	RELIGION AND RATIONAL CHOICE
Robert Young	FREEDOM, RESPONSIBILITY AND GOD

Moral Scepticism

CLEMENT DORE

Professor of Philosophy
Vanderbilt University
Tennessee

MACMILLAN

First published 1991

Published by
MACMILLAN ACADEMIC AND PROFESSIONAL LTD
Houndmills, Basingstoke, Hampshire RG21 2XS
and London
Companies and representatives
throughout the world

Printed in Hong Kong

British Library Cataloguing in Publication Data
Dore, Clement
Moral scepticism.—(Library of philosophy and religion)
1. Ethics. Scepticism
I. Title   II. Series
171.7
ISBN 0–333–53891–9

To Be

Contents

Contents

Preface

In his widely discussed book *Ethics, Inventing Right and Wrong*, J. L. Mackie has set out what he calls 'the argument from queerness'. It goes as follows:

> If there were objective values, then they would be entities or qualities or relations of a very strange sort, utterly different from anything else in the universe. Correspondingly, if we were aware of them, it would have to be by some special faculty of moral perception or intuition, utterly different from our ordinary ways of knowing everything else. . . . [This] central thesis of intuitionism is one to which any objectivist view of values is in the end committed: intuitionism merely makes unpalatably plain what other forms of objectivism wrap up.[1]

Mackie is here calling into question the common-sense view that there are facts, in virtue of which moral judgements are true or false. But more academic moral theories – theories which purport to explain, predict and, to some extent, correct our moral intuitions – are nowadays also under a cloud. Bernard Williams, for example, has recently expressed serious doubts about the adequacy of both Kantian deontologism and utilitarianism.[2]

In roughly the first half of this book, I shall address myself to scepticism regarding our ability to know that some moral judgements are true and some are false. And in Chapters 6–9 I shall deal with the kind of professional moralist's scepticism about morality which Williams voices. I shall assume throughout the book that there is a (Reidian–Moorean–Chisholmian) *prima facie* case against scepticism of any sort. My chief aim is to defend against criticism the thesis that in fact non-sceptical moral theories are available.

ix

I thank the editor of *Philosophical Studies* for permitting me to include in Chapter 8 some material from an article entitled 'Abortion, Some Slippery Slope Arguments and Identity over Time', which appeared in *Philosophical Studies*, vol. 55, no. 3 (March 1989). Chapter 5 of the present book is much like Chapter 5 of my earlier book *God, Suffering and Solipsism* (London: Macmillan, 1989), except that I have made substantial additions to it. I thank Macmillan for allowing the overlap. I also wish to thank my former student Mylan Engel for persuading me that externalist epistemology, which plays an important role in Chapter 4, is not, as I had previously thought, unacceptable.

Finally, I am indebted to James Montmarquet and Hugh Whitaker for some helpful comments on this work while it was in progress.

1 Some Attitude Theories of Morality

1.1 I think that it is obvious that there is no set of moral facts, in virtue of which moral judgements are true or false, which exist wholly independently of the favour or disfavour, being for or against, approval or disapproval of persons. I shall follow the custom of calling moral theories which accept that thesis 'attitude theories', and I shall examine the most prominent of these in this chapter. David Hume, a classical attitude theorist, and contemporary emotivists have given rise to a widespread belief that in fact all attitude theories must be sceptical. It is my intention to show that this is not the case.

In the interest of verbal economy, I shall mostly use 'morally good', 'morally bad' and 'morally evil' to stand for both the moral goodness and badness of persons and – what 'morally right' and 'morally wrong' normally stand for – the moral rightness and wrongness of actions. In Chapter 5, it will be convenient for me to revert to more normal usage.

1.2 Let us look now at the most simple kinds of attitude theories, descriptive and non-descriptive subjectivism. Following A. J. Ayer, we can distinguish two kinds of descriptivist subjectivism.

1 The thesis that 'X is morally good', means 'X is generally approved of' and 'X is morally bad' means 'X is generally disapproved of'.
2 The claim that 'X is morally good' means 'I, the speaker, approve of X' and 'X is morally bad' means 'I, the

speaker, disapprove of X'.[1] I shall call this thesis 'egoistic descriptivist subjectivism'.

Ayer rejects both theses on the ground that one can say without self-contradiction, 'I know that X is generally approved of, but X is not morally good', and that one can also say without self-contradiction, 'I sometimes approve of what is morally bad.'[2] (Ayer does not explicitly add that one can say without self-contradiction, 'I sometimes disapprove of what is morally good', but he would no doubt agree that it would not be self-contradictory for a person to say that. For he plainly wants to rule out, via his self-contradiction test, *all* versions of descriptivist subjectivism.)

None the less, what Ayer replaces descriptivist subjectivism with renders Ayer himself a kind of subjectivist, albeit a *non-descriptivist* subjectivist. His emotivist theory of moral discourse essentially involves the claim that, though moral utterances do not *report* that the speaker has a pro or con attitude toward X, they *evince or display* such an attitude, in the way that a grimace evinces or displays pain without *reporting* that the person who grimaces is in pain.[3]

This theory is obviously a close relative of egoistic descriptivist subjectivism. And it follows that Ayer is guilty of a kind of inconsistency. For, if Ayer's emotivism is correct, and if his defence of it is sound, then one who says, for example, 'Stealing is morally bad, but I don't disfavour it' is doing something which is relevantly similar to saying, 'Ouch, but I'm not in pain' or 'Hurrah for Jones, though I'm not at all favourably disposed toward Jones.' These latter utterances are not, strictly speaking, self-contradictory, but they embody a radical misuse of 'Ouch' and 'Hurrah'. And, if Ayer agreed that, for example, 'Stealing is morally bad, but I don't disfavour it' is also linguistically defective, then he would need to take much more seriously than he does the descriptivist claim that the *kind* of misuse of language which is embodied in such utterances is in fact best construed as logical inconsistency.

But, in any case, just as it is (as Ayer contends) obvious that there is no logical inconsistency involved in saying, for example, 'I know that X is the morally best thing for you to do, but I disfavour your doing it', it is equally clear that there are contexts in which utterances of the envisaged kind embody no linguistic oddness of *any* sort. Consider, for example, 'I know that for you to confess to the crime is the morally best thing for you to do, but, since I very much want you to stay out of prison, I strongly disfavour your confessing.' Ayer adds to his non-descriptivist account of moral language the claim that moral discourse is sometimes used to issue commands (as in 'It is your duty to do it') and suggestions (as in 'It would be a good thing for you to do').[4] But this prescriptivist variety of non-descriptivism is also unacceptable. 'I suppose that it is your duty to rescue him, but, since I strongly desire you to avoid danger, I strongly advise you not to attempt it' is obviously a perfectly acceptable locution, though 'Do it but don't do it' is not. Moreover, suppose that I say, 'It is everyone's duty to save fuel.' This, too, is unexceptionable; but 'Everyone save fuel' is not, unless all the people to whom I am issuing the command are part of my audience. And, of course, the former locution is unexceptionable, whether or not that condition obtains.[5]

1.3 In an article entitled 'Ethical Supernaturalism', which appeared in *Sophia* in October 1976, I maintained that X's being morally obligatory for a given person, S, might well be the same as God's being disposed to disapprove of S's failure to do X,

where the connection between X's being obligatory for S and X's being such that God [is disposed to disapprove of S's failure to do X] is like the connection between a given volume of water and the swarm of H_2O molecules with which it is identical, and, if ... materialists like Smart and Armstrong are right, like the connection between a given [sensory experience] and the brain process with which it is identical.[6]

Let us call such a connection[7] 'a non-semantic identity'. (Examples of semantic identities are the identity which holds between being a biological brother and being a male sibling and the identity which holds between being a square and being an equilateral rectangle.) More recently, a number of philosophers have concluded that moral concepts are best explicated in the envisaged manner.[8]

Here the question arises of what we normally *mean* when we engage in moral discourse. It will not do to maintain that by, for example, 'It is morally bad for S to do X' we mean, say, 'S's doing X causes pain', since causing pain is obviously *not* non-semantically identical with other properties which a philosopher might wish to equate with X's being morally bad – say, God's being disposed to disapprove of X. (Though, of course, S's causing pain by doing X might *cause* God to disapprove of S's doing X.)

However, similar considerations do *not* apply to the thesis that by 'X is morally bad' we normally mean 'X possesses a property in virtue of which "morally bad" is true of it'. For there is nothing to prevent the philosopher who advocates *that* thesis from non-sementically identifying that property with some other property, such as that of being disapproved of by God. And so, too, for 'X is morally good'. If we define it by 'X possesses a property in virtue of which "morally good" is true of it', then it is open to us to view theorizing about the nature of moral goodness as an essentially non-semantical enterprise.

1.4 The present approach to moral concepts protects not only moral supernaturalism from Ayer-like objections, but descriptivist subjectivism as well. The falsity of non-semantic descriptivist subjectivism no more follows from the fact that one can, without logical inconsistency, say, for example, 'X is morally bad but it is neither generally disapproved of nor disapproved of by the speaker' than the falsity of, say, 'This volume of water is a swarm of H_2O molecules' follows from the fact that it is not self-contradictory to deny it. (Ayer's non-descriptivist subjectivism does not fare as well, however. For, if it really is the case that moral language is not fact-stating, then *a fortiori* it is false that moral language ascribes a property which is non-semantically identical with being generally approved of or with being approved of by the speaker.)

Still, even the non-semantic version of descriptivist subjectivism can be seen to be unacceptable. Consider first non-egoistic descriptivist subjectivism. And suppose that X's being morally good is non-semantically identical with X's being generally approved of. Then the moral reformer, who typically says, 'I know that most people approve of X, but X is morally bad', would be like a person who says, 'I know that this is a volume of water, but it is not a swarm of H_2O molecules' – i.e. the former, like the latter, would be, though not logically inconsistent, none the less mistaken. However, it is surely very implausible that anyone who morally opposes something which is generally approved of is *ipso facto* making a mistake.

The egoistic descriptivist subjectivist claim that X's being morally good is non-semantically identical with the approval of X by the person who says 'X is morally good' is also unacceptable, since it entails – what is obviously false – that, whenever I approve of X at time t, and know at t that I do so, and believe at t that X is morally good, then, if I subsequently come to think that I was mistaken at t, I am *ipso facto* wrong. And a similar consideration holds with respect to my *disapproving* of X at time t and my believing at t that X is morally bad.

Finally, both versions of descriptivist subjectivism are incomplete in a very important respect. They do not, as they stand, explain the difference between a specifically *moral* value judgement and a *non*-moral value judgement. Rock music's being generally approved of or being approved of by me is clearly *not* the same as rock music being *morally* good; and a similar consideration holds with respect to disapproval of rock music. I shall return to the topic of specifically *moral* value judgements in Chapter 10.

1.5 Let us define 'an Ideal Observer (an "IO", for short) with respect to the question of whether something, X, is morally good or bad' as 'a person who is impartial and vividly imaginative with respect to X and acquainted with all the empirical[9] facts on which any rational, impartial, vividly imaginative person would, if he knew them, base his judgement of X's moral status'. And let us consider the theory (which I shall call the 'IOT') that the moral badness of X is, roughly speaking,[10] non-semantically identical with X's being such that an IO would – or does – disapprove of X, and that the moral goodness of X consists, roughly speaking,[11] in X's being such that an IO would – or does – approve of X. (In Chapter 4, I shall argue that 'does' is appropriate in these contexts.) In fact, this is only an incomplete account of the IOT, since it does not *per se* enable us to account for specifically moral, as opposed to non-moral, value. However, for simplicity, I shall be dealing with this incomplete characterization until Chapter 10. As we shall see, no harm will come of that.

The IOT does not suffer from the defects of descriptivist subjectivism. First, it does not have the unacceptable consequence that, if I disapproved of X at time t and knew that I did so at t, then at t I could not have been mistaken about X's moral goodness or badness. It entails only the much less implausible thesis that, if I disapproved of X at t *and I was an IO at t*, then I was not apt to be mistaken about X's moral status. The IOT can also accommodate the moral reformer. It follows from the IOT only that, in claiming that X is morally bad (or good), the IO is claiming in effect that X is, or would be, disapproved (or approved) of *by IOs, not* by people generally, and, in particularly, not by *non*-IO's.

1.6 A standard objection to ethical supernaturalism is that God's attitudes cannot be sufficient for moral goodness and badness, since (1) it is possible that God loves cruelty, even when it occurs in circumstances in which it is not the case that the only alternative to it is so bad that it outweighs the negative value of cruelty; (2) it is possible that God hates kindness, even in cases in which the absence of kindness serves no good end; and (3) it is *not* possible for cruelty to be morally good in the former circumstances and for kindness to be morally bad in the latter circumstances. (For simplicity, I shall henceforth drop the qualifiers). Though the following has been overlooked, such a criticism, if sound, applies to other attitude theories as well. Thus, it might be argued that non-egoistic subjectivism must be false, since (a) it is possible that most people approve of cruelty and disapprove of kindness, but (b) it is *not* possible that cruelty is morally good and kindness is morally bad. And egoistic subjectivism is subject to a similar criticism – namely, that it is not possible for, say, cruelty to be morally good, even though it is possible that an individual favours it. Finally, it looks as if the envisaged argument undermines the IOT as well. For it looks as though it is possible for an IO to love cruelty and hate kindness, even though it is not possible that the former is morally good, and the latter morally bad.

Now, I think this objective can be overcome, but only as a part of a lengthy defence of the IOT. I shall return to the objection in 4.6.

1.7 Here another objection may be raised:

> While the IOT avoids the absurd conclusion that intro-
> spective people cannot make mistaken moral judgements,
> it has just the opposite consequence: if the IOT is true,
> then one's moral judgements can *never* be justified.
> For, unless we have reason to believe that *different* IOs
> would not exhibit *conflicting* attitudes towards something,
> X, either we have no reason to make *any* moral judge-
> ment about X or we must accept the radically relativist
> thesis that X is both morally good and morally bad and
> neither (since some IOs may be indifferent). An alterna-
> tive is that a person who finds himself, say, disapproving
> of X, when he is well-informed, impartial and vividly
> imaginative, makes a justified inductive generalization to
> the effect that, since *he* is an IO and disapproves of X, *any*
> *other* IO there might be would *also* disapprove of X. But
> in fact that generalization might well be demonstrably
> unwarranted. (Consider, for example, the conflicting atti-
> tudes which qualified moral judges exhibit toward
> threatening massive nuclear retaliation.) It follows that
> the advocate of the IOT owes us an explanation of why
> the envisaged inductive inference is sound in *some* cases
> but not in *all* cases. And the best that he can do in this
> regard is to maintain (1) that there are *degrees* of know-
> ledge of relevant facts, impartiality and vivid imaginative-
> ness; (2) that all conflicts between moral judgements are
> explicable in terms of different degrees of these qualifica-
> tions; and, hence, (3) that induction with respect to pro or
> con attitudes is sound *when we are dealing with equally*
> *qualified judges*. But is it really reasonable to suppose that
> *all* moral disagreement can be thus accounted for? Can we
> really be sure that all equally qualified judges would agree
> about, say, the threat of nuclear retaliation? Surely, the
> answer is that we cannot. So, we are owed *another* answer
> to the question of why we should trust *some*, but not *all*, of

the envisaged inductive inferences. And, until (what is unlikely) such an explanation is forthcoming, we are entitled to hold that the IOT cannot overcome moral scepticism.[12]

Before answering this objection, I shall begin a lengthy defence of a version of the IOT. I shall return to the objection in 4.4.

2 A Proof of the Existence of God

2.1 In Meditation Five, Descartes argues that 'there is not any less repugnance to our conceiving a God (that is, a Being supremely perfect) to whom existence is lacking (that is to say, to whom a certain perfection is lacking) than to conceive of a mountain which has no valley'. And he draws the conclusion that 'existence is inseparable from Him, and hence He really exists'.[1]

Alvin Plantinga[2] imposes the following interpretation on Descartes-like arguments:

> (1) the concept of God . . . includes existence; but then (2) it will be necessarily false that God does not exist, and hence (3) it is necessarily true that God does exist.

Plantinga rejects this type of argument on the grounds that (a), 'given step (1), what follows at step (2) is only that it is not possible that the concept of God be exemplified by a thing that does not exist', and (b), though (2) is plainly true, it is clear that (3) does not follow from it.

However, there appears to be another, more charitable interpretation of Descartes's argument.

1   The concept of God is the concept of a perfect being who is supremely perfect, in the sense that he possesses all those properties which are such that it is better than not that a perfect being should possess them.[3]
2   The concept of existence is the concept of such a property.

Hence

3   the concept of God stands to the concept of existence as

11

the concept of a mountain stands to the concept of a valley.[4]

So

4 it is a conceptual truth that God exists, i.e. we can discover that 'God exists' expresses a truth simply by reflecting on the concepts of God and of existence.
5   The concept of God is such that 'God exists' does not just express the ontologically insignificant truth that, if God exists, then he exists.

But

6 'Nothing is both God and yet fails to exist' (roughly speaking, Plantinga's interpretation) means 'It is false both that God exists and does not exist', which is logically equivalent to 'If God exists, then he exists.'

So

7 'God exists' does not mean the same thing as 'Nothing is both God and yet fails to exist' and *a fortiori* it does not make the ontologically sterile, conditional assertion that, if God exists, then he exists.

Step 5 is, of course, crucial and is obviously in need of defence. One such defence is just that, if step 5 is false, then, contrary to appearances, steps 1–3 are not epistemically relevant to the claim that 'God exists' expresses a truth, since we clearly have no need of *grounds* for the proposition that, if God exists, then he exists. This is not, perhaps, a *very* compelling reason for accepting step 5. But the following is another, stronger defence.

2.2 Let us say that, for any value of X, 'X has actual existence' means that the sentence '*X* exists' (1) expresses a truth and (2) is not equivalent in meaning to any vacuous conditional sentence. Then we can rephrase the envisaged argument as follows.

(i)   The concept of God is the concept of a being who possesses all those properties which are such that it is better than not that a perfect being possesses them.

(ii) The concept of actual existence is the concept of such a property.

So

(iii) it is a conceptual truth that God has actual existence.

Hence

(iv) God has actual existence.

Now it looks to be plainly false that all that *this* argument establishes is the ontologically sterile conclusion that, if God exists, then he exists. For it appears that what it shows, if it is sound, is precisely the opposite. Hence, it looks as though the present argument shows that the argument of 2.1 (call it *O*) is sound.

Here someone may say,

'God' means in part 'being who has actual existence'. So 'God has actual existence' analytically entails, 'A being who has actual existence has actual existence.' And this sentence clearly means 'If God exists, then he has actual existence.' Otherwise, we could prove the existence of, say, winged horses by arguing that 'Actually existent winged horses have actual existence' is not reducible to the ontologically sterile sentence 'If actually existent winged horses exist, then they have actual existence.' But, if 'God has actual existence' means 'If God exists, then he has actual existence', then the former sentence expresses a proposition which is comptible with its being the case that 'God exists' means 'If God exists, then he exists.' So the revised argument does not after all show that *O* has ontological significance.

But the objection can easily be met. One reply to it as follows: it is clear that, if 'God has actual existence' does not express a true proposition which is incompatible with its being the case that 'God exists' means 'If God exists, then he exists', then no sentence does. So my opponent is arguing in effect that the concept of God is such that it is not possible to express a true proposition which is incompatible with its being the case that 'God exists' means the same as 'If God exists, then he exists.' But this can be seen to be wrong.

By 'a *C* concept' let us mean 'a concept of something, *X*, such that it is possible to express a true proposition about *X* which is incompatible with its being the case that "*X* exists" means the same as "If *X* exists, then it exists."' And consider the following argument.

(i) The concept of God is the concept of a supremely perfect being.
(ii) The concept of a supremely perfect being is a *C* concept.

So

(iii) the concept of God is a *C* concept.

Now,

(iv) if the sentence 'God has actual existence' does not express a true proposition which is incompatible with its being the case that 'God exists' means the same as 'If God exists, then he exists', then no sentence does.

But,

(v)   if the sentence 'God has actual existence' means the same as 'If God exists, then he has actual existence' (call this sentence *S*), then the proposition which is expressed by the former sentence is not incompatible with its being the case that 'God exists' means the same as 'If God exists, then he exists.'

Hence

(vi)   'God has actual existence' does not mean the same as *S*.

So

(vii)   it is after all true that the revised argument shows that 'God exists' does not mean the same as 'If God exists, then he exists.'

A second reply to the envisaged objection is this: let us mean by '*X* has real actual existence' that the sentence '*X* has actual existence' is (1) true and (2) not equivalent in meaning to any ontologically sterile conditional sentence. And consider the following argument.

(i)   The concept of God is the concept of a supremely perfect being.
(ii)   The concept of real actual existence is the concept of a perfection relative to a perfect being.

Hence

(iii)   it is a conceptual truth that God has real actual existence.

So

(iv)   God has real actual existence.

What this argument shows is that 'God has actual existence' expresses the non-ontologically-sterile truth that 'God exists' expresses a non-ontologically-sterile truth. Or, at any rate, the contemplated argument establishes this unless 'God has real actual existence' means 'If God, a being who has real actual existence, exists, then he has real actual existence.' But, if anyone maintains that in fact this is the case, then his objection can be countered by (a) introducing the concept of X's having actual real actual existence – of X's being such that the sentence 'X has real actual existence' (1) expresses a truth and (2) is not equivalent in meaning to any ontologically sterile conditional sentence – and (b) pointing out that the concept of God stands to the concept of having actual real actual existence as, say, the concept of a square stands to the concept of a figure with more sides than three. It follows from this that 'God has real actual existence' expresses the non-ontologically-sterile truth that 'God has actual existence' expresses the non-ontologically-sterile truth that 'God exists' expresses a non-ontologically sterile truth. And it would surely be preposterous to claim at this point that 'God has actual real actual existence' is equivalent in meaning to 'If God, a being who has actual real actual existence, exists, then he has actual real actual existence.' And, as the regress that we are started on progresses, claims of the envisaged sort would become more and more incredible.

But what is the alternative? Consider the following argument:

Since O purports to establish that it is a conceptual truth that God exists, and a conceptual truth that God has actual existence, and real actual existence, and so on, it in effect purports to establish that all of these propositions are necessary truths. But all necessary truths are analytic truths, and all analytic truths are reducible to conditional truths. Thus, 'Squares are four-sided' is a necessary-*cum-*

analytic truth. And it means the same as '*If* anything is a square, *then* it is four-sided.' Otherwise, for example, 'Centaurs are half horses and half humans', which expresses a necessary-*cum*-analytic truth, should, in consistency, *not* be construed as meaning '*If* anything is a centaur, *then* it is half horse and half human', and we should have to include centaurs in our ontology. Hence, since 'God exists', 'God has actual existence', and so on, are necessary-*cum*-analytic truths, they *are* in fact reducible to 'If God exists, then he exists', 'If God exists, then he has actual existence', and so on. So we shall simply have to countenance the envisaged regress.

The reply to this argument is that it is false that all necessary truths are analytic. In medieval terminology, some are *de re*, rather than *de dicto*, true.

The following is an explication of that claim. Consider the *de dicto*, necessary truth that square objects are equilateral rectangular objects. Plainly it does not follow from that truth that any given square object is such that it is broadly logically impossible that it is not an equilateral rectangular object, but, say, a round object instead. For square objects are such that it is broadly logically possible that they are not *square* objects but, for example, round objects instead. Again, though it is *de dicto* necessary that bachelors are unmarried (etc.) males, any given bachelor is such that it is broadly logically possible that he is not an unmarried male but a married one instead. For bachelors are such that it is broadly logically possible that they are not *bachelors* but married men instead.

Consider, however, the time-relativized predicates 'is a square object at moment *M*' and 'is a round object at moment *M*'. As every student of modal logic knows, though it is broadly logically possible that a given object, *X*, is a square object at *M* and it is also broadly logically possible that *X* is a round object at *M*, it is not broadly logically possible that X is *both* a square object *and* a round object at M. Examples can be multiplied indefinitely. Thus, though it is broadly logically possible that X is red all over at M and it is broadly logically possible that X is green all over at M, it is *not* broadly logically possible that X is *both* red all over *and* green all over at M; though it is broadly logically possible that X is red all over at M and it is broadly logically possible that X is not red all over at M, it is not broadly logically possible that X is *both* red all over and not red all over at M. Nor are such time-relativized predicates the *only* ones in terms of which the *de dicto/de re* distinction can be explained. Consider, for example, the *de re* necessary truth that President Bush will remain a non-number for as long as he exists. Here, again, it is plainly false that it is broadly logically possible that President Bush is not a non-number, since it is not broadly logically possible that he is not President Bush, but, say, the number 9 instead.

In short, what I am maintaining is that the claim that it is broadly logically possible that God does not exist is strongly similar to the claim that it is broadly logically possible that X is both a square object and a round object at a given moment, M, and that it is broadly logically possible that President Bush is not in fact President Bush but, say, the square root of 4. But this means that the conclusion of O cannot be reducible to the vacuous, non-perfection-ascribing claim that, if God exists, then he exists. And that in turn entails that 'God has actual existence', and similar statements, are not so reducible.

2.3 Here my critic may object as follows.

Dore himself has in effect been claiming that it is true that God has actual existence, real actual existence, actual real actual existence, and so on *ad infinitum*. Now Dore maintains that God has these properties with *de re*, rather than *de dicto*, necessity. But surely Dore's *de re* regress is not any less unpalatable than my *de dicto* regress.

One reply to this objection is that in fact the *de dicto* regress is much more implausible than the putative *de re* regress, inasmuch as the former regress, unlike the latter, involves claims to the effect that 'God' is in part *synonymous with*, for example, 'being who has real actual real actual (etc.) existence'; and these claims are obviously false.

But, even if we set that consideration aside, there is another reply to the envisaged objection: namely, that I am *not* committed to an infinite *de re* regress. Suppose that 'God exists' does in fact express a non-vacuous truth. Then *eo ipso* God has *actual* existence. But 'God has actual existence' is logically sufficient for 'God has real actual existence.' For that latter sentence unpacks as follows: 'The sentence "The sentence 'God exists' expresses a non-vacuous truth" expresses a non-vacuous truth.' And it is possible for the entire sentence to be false only if the innermost sentence is false: if 'God exists' expresses a non-vacuous truth, then the claim that it does so also expresses a non-vacuous truth. And similar considerations hold for real actual existence and actual real actual existence. Having the former is broadly logically sufficient for having the latter. And so, too, for any adjacent pair of sentences with which one could extend the regress. But broadly logical sufficiency is transitive. Hence '"God exists" expresses a non-vacuous truth' is broadly logically sufficient for any member of the regress.

But if 'S has property P_1' is broadly logically sufficient for 'S has property P_2', then we need not conclude that 'S has property P_2' is true in virtue of S's possessing some property which is distinct from P_1. (Thus 'S is walking' is broadly logically sufficient for 'S is moving his legs.' And, if S is indeed walking, then S's moving his legs is not a property which is distinct from his walking.)

It follows that I am entitled to break off the regress at the point at which my critic grows weary. For the fact that, if I were to formulate further members of the series, then they would be true, does not entail that God in fact possesses some properties, in virtue of which they would be true, and which are distinct from his possessing those properties, in virtue of which it is true just that 'God exists' expresses a non-conditional, ontologically significant truth.

2.4   Consider the following, very familiar analysis of existence claims (call it *A*): 'Cows exist' means 'Some things are cows'; 'Dinosaurs existed' means 'Some things were dinosaurs'; and so on. If *A* is correct, then *O* is unsound, for *O* entails that existence is one of God's perfections, and that entails in turn that existence is a property of things, i.e. that 'exists' is a descriptive predicate; and, given *A*, we do not attribute the property of existence to cows, etc., when we say that they exist. Rather, we attribute the property of being a cow (a dinosaur, etc.) to some things.

But, while *A* looks very plausible with respect to such sentences as 'Cows exist', it looks considerably less plausible when we turn to sentences in which 'exists' is in the predicate place, but where the subject term is a proper name, such as 'George Bush'. For, since it is very doubtful that there is such a property as being George Bush, it is also very doubtful that proper names such as 'George Bush' are descriptive terms. With some exceptions to be discussed shortly, it looks very much as though any sentence of the form 'George Bush is *P*', where *P* is some non-vacuous predicate, expresses a contingent truth or a contingent falsehood. Thus it is only *contingently* false that George Bush died as a child. And that would not be the case if a credible explication of 'George Bush' contained 'lived into his sixties'. And, again, it is only contingently false that George Bush lost the 1988 presidential election. And that would not be so if 'George Bush' *meant* in part 'winner of the 1988 presidential election'. Of course, it is *not* just contingently true that George Bush is not both a human being and a non-human being. But surely 'not both human and non-human' is not part of what is *meant* by 'George Bush'. A predicate which is not (quite) vacuous is 'a non-number'. And the statement that 'George Bush' is a non-number is not just contingently true. But this is not because 'George Bush is a non-number' expresses a *de dicto*, rather than a *de re*, necessary truth: 'being a non-number' would not be yielded by any credible explication of 'George Bush'.

Similar considerations apply to Saul Kripke's controversial claim that it is a necessary truth that any given person came from such and such a fertilized ovum. If Kripke is right, then we have here a case of *de re*, rather than *de dicto* necessity. For surely 'George Bush' cannot be correctly explicated by 'came from a certain fertilized ovum'. If it could, then, since most of us do not know what that fertilized ovum was, either most of us do not know what 'George Bush' means, or (just as bad) all proper names, barring only those with respect to which we have detailed knowledge of the biological origins of their bearers, have the same meaning.

But *could* George Bush have been, say, the discoverer of the positron or a twelfth-century pope? Isn't the claim that he has *those* properties necessarily false? I think that the answer is 'Yes', but, once again, we have *de re*, rather than *de dicto*, necessity here. For 'George Bush' surely cannot be adequately explicated as 'among other things, not the discoverer of the positron and not a twelfth-century pope'.

Still, there may be a lingering doubt. For 'This is George Bush' is a perfectly acceptable locution, which has 'George Bush' in the predicate, rather than the subject, place. But there are plausible alternatives to the claim that 'George Bush' is a descriptive term in the envisaged sentence. I have in mind the following explications: (1) 'This person is called

"George Bush" '; (2) 'This is the person typically referred to by the name "George Bush"', or 'This is the person who is typically referred to by people whom you have seen or heard use the name "George Bush".'

Here it may be said, 'There is a plausible analysis of "George Bush exists" which is an extension of A (call it A_2), i.e. "Some thing is identical with George Bush", where the "is" is the "is" of identity rather than of predication.' But the envisaged analysans is equivalent to ' "George Bush" is such that some thing is identical with him'; and this latter sentence ascribes to George Bush the property of being identical with some thing. It follows that the present proposal is equivalent to the thesis that the property of existence can be plausibly explicated as the property of being identical with some thing. Now I think that 'identical', in this context, is sufficiently obscure for there to be a gain in clarity if we explicate 'X has the property of being identical with some thing' by 'X has the property of existence', rather than *vice versa*. But, whether or not I am right in so thinking, O remains essentially unaffected. For, if the critic of that argument agrees that existence is a property, though a property which is most perspicuously expressed by a given expression, E, other than 'existence', then we can simply replace 'existence', wherever it occurs in O, with E, and point out that, if the contemplated analysis is correct, then the new version of O is just as likely to be sound as is the old one. (Since I know of no property expression, E, which illuminates the property of existence to a greater extent than does 'existence', I shall in what follows continue to formulate O in terms of existence.)

2.5 But now consider the following argument.

If 'P' is a descriptive predicate, then 'not-P' is descriptive as well. So, if 'exist' is a descriptive predicate, then so is 'do not exist'. But, for example, 'Centaurs do not exist' expresses a truth. And, if sentences of the form 'S is P' are descriptive utterances and express a truth, then P is true of S. So, since 'Centaurs do not exist' expresses a truth, 'do not exist' is true of something, namely centaurs, given that 'exist' and, hence, 'do not exist' are descriptive. It follows from the claim that 'exist' is descriptive, then, that there are non-existent objects; and surely this is a conclusion which it is best to avoid if at all possible. (It does not follow from the denial of non-existent objects that there are no possible worlds in which there are objects that are distinct from any individuals in the actual world, only that, in quantifying over those worlds, we do not quantify over those objects.)

One response to this argument is that, in the absence of a plausible explantion of how 'exists' can fail to be descriptive in for example, 'George Bush exists', we should conclude that 'exists' and 'do not exist' are exceptions to the claim (call it T) that, if P is descriptive, then so is 'not-P'. But there is a more plausible reply – namely that we speak *misleadingly* when we say 'Centaurs do not exist.' We should, when doing philosophy, replace that sentence with 'It is not the case that centaurs exist.' The former sentence is, of course, *syntactically* correct, but, unlike the second sentence, it is semantically flawed: strictly speaking, it is false. Hence, we do not have here a *bona fide* exception to T. Though 'do not exist' is a descriptive term, there is nothing for it to describe. This conclusion would, of course, be unacceptable if there were no paraphrase of 'Centaurs do not exist' which is ontologically innocent. But, once again, there is such a paraphrase: namely, 'It is not the case that centaurs exist.'[5]

2.6 The reader may well ask here whether O threatens to overwhelm us by generating an indefinitely large number of supremely perfect beings. Moreover, it may well be objected here that an *O*-like argument generates the existence of *nearly* supremely perfect beings, since the concept of existence would surely be the concept of a perfection in a being who is only slightly surpassed, with respect to his perfections, by a *completely* supremely perfect being. A theistic resolution of both of these problems will be presented in 4.4 and 4.5.

3 Agnosticism and the Atheistic Argument from Suffering

3.1 A very familiar argument against the existence of a supremely perfect being can be put as follows. Such a being would be omnipotent and, hence, would have the power to prevent suffering; and he would also be perfectly morally good and so would want to do so. It follows that there is no being who combines omnipotence and perfect moral goodness and, hence, that God does not exist. If this argument (call it A) is sound, then, since its conclusion contradicts the conclusion of O, the latter must be unsound; and, of course, the converse is true: if O is sound, then A is unsound.

Now, it may look as if it is simple matter to show that it is O, rather than A, which is in fact sound. It may be said that the perfect goodness of God is not impugned by suffering, since, for all the atheist can prove to the contrary, there is an enormously valuable state of affairs (call it E) which is sufficiently valuable to outweigh the negative value of the suffering which the universe contains, and which, since it is a necessary truth that it could not exist in the absence of that suffering, is such that even an omnipotent being could not bring it about unless that suffering occurred.

What other relation does suffering bear to E? The claim that suffering is a cause of E is unacceptable. For it is similar to the claim that, for example, heating water to boiling-point causes tornadoes. This claim is obviously false, and the reason is the strong observational evidence against it: we have often witnessed the heating of water to boiling-point but have never observed an appropriately conjoined tornado. But, by the same token, we have observed instances of

suffering on many occasions and have never observed anything like an appropriate constant conjunction between
them and *E*. And, by parity of reasoning, we should
conclude that we have observational evidence against the
claim that suffering causes *E*.

But there is a more plausible alternative: 'Though suffering does not *cause E*, it is entailed by something, *S*, which
both causes *E* and is such that it is a necessary truth that *E*
could not exist in its absence. And, since the operation of
scientific laws on whatever matter may exist entails
suffering,[1] this is the candidate that best fits that description
of *S*. Call, for simplicity, the operation of scientific laws on
whatever matter may exist 'the empirical universe'. Then
this rebuttal is significantly unlike the claim that, for all the
atheist can prove to the contrary, instances of suffering
cause *E*. For, though we have empirical evidence that the
latter is false, since we have observed many instances of
suffering and have never observed an appropriate conjunction of those instances with *E*, we have *not* observed more
than one empirical universe and *a fortiori* it is false that we
have observed *many* empirical universes and have never
observed an appropriate conjunction of them with *E*.

Still, there is a further problem. Consider the following
parody of my rebuttal of *A*:

Though we have observational evidence that boiling water
does not *cause* tornadoes, it may be, for all that anyone
can prove to the contrary, that boiling water is none the
less connected with tornadoes in the following manner: *S*
entails *both* boiling water *and* tornadoes, not just *empirical*
tornadoes, but *extra*-empirical tornadoes as well.

The reply to this argument is, of course, that, even though
(it is a tautology that) we do not have observational evidence
against extra-empirical tornadoes, we are none the less not
warranted in positing extra-empirical tornadoes in the

absence of some (empirical or non-empirical) evidence for them. And, barring evidence for *it*, the same holds true of *E*.

Here it will be said that, though we have no reason to believe in extra-empirical *tornadoes*, we do in fact have a ground for believing in *E*: namely, argument *O* of Chapter 2. But now still another problem arises. Suppose that the theist argues here as follows:

> In view of *O*, *A* establishes *only* that *either* (1) God does not exist *or* (2) *E* exists. Now *O* is evidence for the falsity of (1) and, hence, is *eo ipso* evidence for the truth of (2).

A little reflection will show that this argument is no more cogent than the following one:

> Jones's wife sometimes gives him evidence that she (always) loves him, and sometimes gives him evidence that she (always) does not. But, in view of the evidence that she loves him, the evidence that she does not indicates *only* that *either* (1) she doesn't love Jones *or* (2) she only pretends on occasion not to love him. And the evidence that she loves him is in effect evidence that (1) is false and, hence, that (2) is true.

It is plain that this argument is fallacious: the evidence that his wife loves Jones may not be used *twice over*, first in order to prove that the evidence *against* her loving Jones does not establish that she does not love Jones *simpliciter* but only the weaker claim that *either* (1) she does not love Jones *or* (2) she only pretends on occasion not to love Jones; secondly to rule out (1). And the former argument suffers from an exactly similar defect. It asserts, rightly, that, in view of *O*, the atheist is not entitled to make the strong claim that suffering shows that God does not exist *simpliciter* but only the weaker claim that *either* (1) God does not exist *or* (2) *E* exists. But it also illegitimately uses *O* twice over, first to show that the atheist is entitled to infer from *A* only the contemplated (weak) disjunction, and secondly to show that disjunct (1) is false.

Now it may well look here as though the aspiring theist needs some way of proving that *O* constitutes stronger evidence for the falsity of (1) than suffering does for its truth and that, barring such evidence, he must, if he is to be rational, suspend judgement about theism. (Similarly it may look as if Jones should suspend judgement about his wife's affections unless he can show that the evidence that she loves him is stronger than the evidence that she does not.) But is that really so?

3.2 Suppose that the agnostic argues as follows that his position is superior:

> The person who claims that it is not known whether a given proposition, *p*, is true does not bear the same onus of proof as does the person who claims to know that *p* is true and the person who claims to know that *p* is false. And, since a person who claims to know that theism is true is confronted with the atheistic argument from suffering, he cannot *adequately* shoulder his burden of proving that theism is true, even if he presents some reasonably plausible argument for that position. But, by the same token, the atheist cannot adequately shoulder his burden (by advancing the argument from suffering), because of argument *O*. It follows that simply refusing to shoulder any burden at all in this area is the most rational thing to do.

So goes the agnostic's argument. Now, one part of it is very plausible: namely, the claim that for any proposition, *p*, there is an onus of proof on the person who claims that it is known that *p* is true (or false) which does not rest on the person who denies this. Thus, the person who claims that it is known that there is life on Mars is epistemically obliged to adduce evidence for his claim, even if there is no evidence that there is no life on Mars, while it is surely false that the person who claims that it is *not* known that there is life on Mars is equally epistemically obliged to adduce evidence for his position, if there is no evidence that there is life there.

But now consider the following three alternatives.

(1) There is more evidence for theism than for atheism.
(2) There is more evidence for atheism than for theism.
(3) There is the same – or almost the same – amount of evidence for both positions.

In claiming that it is not known whether theism or atheism is true, the agnostic can be taken to be doing one of two things with respect to (1), (2) and (3): (a) maintaining that (3) is true; (b) maintaining that it is not known whether (1) or (2) or (3) is true. But, if the agnostic is doing the former thing, then, though he is suspending judgement with respect to theism and atheism and, hence, avoiding the onus of having to show that either of those positions is true he is *not* suspending judgement with respect to (3), and, hence, he must accept a certain onus: namely, that of showing that (3) is true. And it is unlikely that he is prepared to do so.

But suppose that the agnostic agrees that we ought to suspend judgement about whether (1) or (2) or (3) is true. Then he will no longer be able legitimately to claim superiority for his position. For he would be the first to agree that, since we do not know that (1) is true, it is false that theism is more rational than atheism and agnosticism; and, since we do not know that (2) is true, it is false that atheism is more rational than theism and agnosticism. And why, then, should he refuse to accept the analogous conclusion that, since we do not know that (3) is true, it is false that agnosticism is more rational than either theism or atheism?

There is an answer which he might wish to give here:

> We cannot agree that there is good reason to reject theism, atheism *and* agnosticism; for we must adopt one of these positions: there is no fourth alternative. And it cannot be true that we are irrational no matter which position we opt for. But, that being so, a suspension of judgement regarding theism and atheism is surely the most rational course. Consider an analogous case. In the present state of scientific knowledge, it is not clear whether or not there is intelligent extraterrestrial life. Or, at any rate, let us assume, for the sake of furthering the argument, that this is so. And let us also assume (what may well be the case) that there is not plainly more evidence for one of the following alternatives than for another: (1') The thesis (call it *TH*) that there is intelligent, extraterrestrial life is better evidenced than not-*TH*; (2') Not-*TH* is better evidenced than *TH*; (3') *TH* and not-*TH* are equally well evidenced. But now, even given this assumption, it is surely not just as rational to affirm *TH* or to affirm not-*TH* as to suspend judgement about the matter. Surely a scientist who affirmed or denied *TH* in the envisaged circumstances would be thought to be a very odd scientist indeed.

The reply to this argument is that, though it does sound strange to maintain that affirming or denying *TH* is, in the circumstances, as rational as suspending judgement, this is not because we subscribe to a sound epistemic principle which dictates that we should suspend judgement in such cases, but rather because *we have no motive* for either affirming or denying *TH* and because our psychology is such that, when we are not motivated to affirm or to deny a proposition, we normally do neither. But this is a psychological fact, and epistemic appraisal is out of place here. Moreover, regarding theism, we *do* have a motive for *not* suspending judgement: namely, the consideration that (1) there is a *prima facie* case against moral scepticism (cf. the Preface); (2) as I shall show in the next chapter, theism provides the basis for a defence of a non-sceptical version of the IOT; and (3) it is very far from clear that any other defence of morality is available. (At any rate, if someone denies this, then he owes us an alternative defence.)

3.3 The following is an objection to the central argument in 3.2.

> Dore is trading on the fact that not knowing whether there is more evidence for *p* than for not-*p* and *vice versa* obviously does not entail knowing that there is the same amount of evidence for each. A fundamentalist who is in the early stages of doubt about creationism plainly does not know that there is in fact the same amount of evidence for non-creationism as for creationism. But for the fundamentalist not to know whether *he has* the same amount of evidence for non-creationism as for creationism *does* entail that he knows that *he* has the same amount of evidence for each; and so he is epistemically obliged to suspend judgement. The agnostic does not *need* an independent argument for this.

But this argument is not impressive, since the budding non-fundamentalist could fail to know at time *t* that he had more evidence for non-creationism than for creationism and subsequently discover that he did in fact have more evidence for the former than for the latter at *t*, but, due to prejudice or lazy-mindedness, had simply failed to recognize this at *t*.

It is at least possible, then, for people to have more evidence for *p* than for not-*p* and *vice versa* at a given time and yet fail to recognize that they do. So it is at best a contingent fact that we *normally* have the same amount of evidence for *p* and not-*p* and *vice versa*. But I submit that we are in need of an *argument* that this *is* a fact or, at any rate, that *O* and the argument from suffering, at least, present (reflective) people with the same amount of evidence for theism and atheism; i.e. the onus is, after all, on the agnostic to show that this is in fact the case.

4 A Proof of the Ideal-Observer Theory

4.1 So much for the proof of God's existence. In what follows, I shall argue that God is a supremely perfect Ideal Observer (an SPIO).

4.2 Any person who does not have a pro attitude toward properties such as kindness, honesty and courage would be, in that respect, seriously morally defective. Hence, God, who is morally perfect, has such pro attitudes. Moreover, any person who failed to disapprove of such characteristics as cruelty and greed would, for that reason, be seriously morally defective. So God has such con attitudes. (The question of why in fact there *are* morally bad people and actions to have con attitudes *towards* will be discussed in the next chapter.)

But why should we suppose that God is an SPIO? This reduces to the question of why we should think that all the goodness of, say, kindness amounts to is roughly[1] being loved by God, and all that the badness of, say, cruelty amounts to is roughly[2] being hated by God. And this in turn reduces to the further question of why we should not hold that God favours morally good things *because* they are good and disfavours morally bad things *because* they are bad, rather than that morally good things are good because they are favoured by God and morally bad things are bad because they are disfavoured by God. The answer is that (1) *some* attitude theory is very likely to be correct if *any* moral theory is; (2) as Chapter 1 has made clear, the IOT is a more promising theory than other prominent attitude theories; and, hence, (3) since there is a *prima facie* case against moral scepticism, there is a *prima facie* case on behalf of the thesis that *some* version of the IOT is correct. The criticisms of the IOT which I shall be considering throughout the rest of the chapter should be viewed as attempts to *overcome* that *prima facie* case.

4.3 But first I shall set out a preliminary defence of the claim that radical moral scepticism is false.

In order to do what is morally good, we must have *true beliefs* about what is morally good. Suppose that I think that my doing *X* is doing something heinous, whereas in fact my doing *X would* be morally good, if I did not hold the former belief. Then it is very dubious, given what I do believe, that in doing *X* I do what is morally good. For I would certainly not be *praiseworthy* for doing *X* in the envisaged circumstances.

Similar considerations apply to my doing what is morally bad. Suppose that I believe, through no fault of my own, that my doing *X* is not morally bad, even though, if I did not hold this belief, my doing *X would* be morally bad. Then it is very dubious that by doing *X* I would make myself an object of justified moral disapproval.

Now, a person who can create the opportunity for himself and others to favour kindness, honesty and courage and who brings that opportunity about is *ceteris paribus* more perfect than a person who can create that opportunity but does not in fact do so. Hence, God sees to it that our positive moral judgements are often correct. It is, of course, less clear that a person who creates the opportunity to *disfavour* cruelty and greed is *ceteris paribus* more perfect than a person who does not. But I shall argue in Chapter 5 that in fact God's creating free moral agents and, therefore, the possibility of moral badness is one of his perfections.

It follows that we can know that we *sometimes* make true moral judgements. But, of course, unless we can know *which* moral judgements are the true ones, we cannot be justified objects of praise and blame.

Well, then, which moral judgements *are* the true ones? In view of the *prima facie* case on behalf of the IOT, the most plausible answer is that they are the moral judgements which are based on our favouring or disfavouring something, *X*, *when we are as much like an SPIO as possible with respect to our pro or con attitudes toward X*, i.e. when we are ourselves, to some extent, IOs.

It follows that the correctness of our moral judgements is a function of our taking the trouble to become qualified moral judges. But why does God not make us all IOs like himself, regardless of whether we try to be? A preliminary answer is that a person's freely choosing to be an IO is preferable to his being caused to be one by things over which he has no control. (Again, I shall argue in Chapter 5 that it is in fact good to be able to make such free choices.)

4.4 Here my critic may press his case via the following argument:

If argument *O* (of Chapter 2) is sound, then it establishes the existence of an indefinitely large number of supremely perfect beings. And, though the arguments of 4.2 and 4.3 purport to support the conclusion that each of these beings is an SPIO, they do not show that, for any two SPIO's (SPIO$_1$ and SPIO$_2$) and any given moral agent, *A*, SPIO$_1$ and SPIO$_2$ will always have similar attitudes toward *A* and his actions. Indeed, the fact that *human* IOs sometimes exhibit conflicting attitudes toward human moral agents and their actions gives us reason to believe that different SPIOs often have such conflicting attitudes. So, if the SPIO theory (the SPIOT) is correct, then *A* and his actions are often both morally good and morally bad, and – to accommodate SPIOs who are sometimes indifferent to *A* and his actions – neither morally good nor morally bad. Moreover, it can do human moral judges no epistemic good *vis-à-vis A* to make themselves IOs, since, whether they do so or not, different SPIOs will often have conflicting attitudes towards *A* and his actions. It follows that, though the argument of 4.3 supports the claim that human IOs can often know that a given moral judgement is true, the considerations just presented entail that the SPIOT gives rise to a radical relativism in which *any* human moral judge – whether he is an IO or not – is as likely to be right about *A* and his actions as any other.

The reply to this argument is that the concept of a supremely perfect being (SPB) is such that it is a conceptual truth that (subject to a qualification to be given in 4.11) any SPB would have as one of his perfections its being logically impossible to surpass, or even rival, him with respect to the number and degree of his perfections: any being who lacked that perfection would *eo ipso* fall short of being a *supremely* perfect being. Hence, any SPB would be such that he is the one and only logical possible SPB, i.e. only one (at most) such being is logically possible. The proof of this conclusion is not just that it follows from plausible premises, but that, in view of their plausibility, it is the best explanation of why argument *O* does not commit us to an unacceptably bloated ontology.

Now, *pace* the inductivist of 1.7, it may be that it sometimes happens that equally qualified IOs have conflicting attitudes towards some kinds of actions. (I think that the most plausible candidates are threatening massive nuclear retaliation, and killing large numbers of civilians in wartime bombing-raids, in order to prevent an even larger number of deaths.) But, since, as we have just seen, only one SPIO is logically possible, conflicts between *human* IOs do not support the claim that there may be different and conflicting SPIO attitudes. Moreover, it is false that, in cases in which the putative conflicts occur, there is no fact of the matter.

The SPIO, since he is an SPB, always has the *definitive* pro and con attitudes, as well as definitive indifference on those occasions on which he is indifferent.

Finally, though we cannot, perhaps, tell, in every case of conflicting human attitudes toward X, which moral judge has the SPIO's attitude toward X, it is none the less true that, since it is demonstrable that human beings are very frequently in possession of moral truths (see 4.3), we are at *least for the most part* entitled to hold that human moral conflicts are explicable in terms of detectable, different degrees of IO-hood. Thus we are entitled to hold that human beings who are opposed to abortion under any circumstances have not thought the matter through as carefully as their opponents (I shall argue for this in Chapter 8); that witch-burners were mistaken about whether their activities caused more pain that it prevented;[3] that people who are morally indifferent to inflicting pain on animals for trivial reasons are not really vividly imaginative about animal suffering; that people who are opposed to signing arms-reduction treaties with the Soviets are not really well acquainted with all the relevant facts; that wealthy opponents of bettering the condition of the poor lack impartiality; and so on. And, in any case, we have a good reason for thinking that *most* moral disputes can be rationally settled by qualified moral judges – a reason which would be sadly lacking if *no* version of the IOT were an adequate account of moral knowledge.

4.5   The prior section in effect answers the question (which was raised in 2.6) of whether argument O generates an indefinitely large number of SPBs. We can now see clearly that it does not. Can we also dispose of the objection that argument O generates not only an SPB, but *nearly* supremely perfect beings as well? Here matters are not so simple; for a defender of the envisaged parody may maintain (1) that the concept of a nearly supremely perfect being (an NSPB) is, like the concept of an SPB *simpliciter*, the concept of an essentially unique being; (2) that argument *O* is as apt to generate the existence of an NSPB as it is to generate the existence of an SPB; and, hence, (3) that it would be question-begging to argue that an SPB exists and so it is impossible for an NSPB to exist: the converse is just as likely to be true.

The answer is that the concept of the SPB is such that, *even if it were not instantiated*, no concept of a being who is nearly as perfect as he could possibly be instantiated. Hence, *O* proves the existence of a completely supremely perfect being but not of an NSPB.

By parity of reasoning, we should expand *O* to include this premise: 'There is no good reason to think that the concept of an SPB is logically incoherent.' Anyone who can adduce such a reason can *ipso facto* refute *O*. But I submit that, to date, no such reason has been presented.

Here someone may say, 'We should also add to *O* the premise that an SPB *is* in fact logically possible. And then it will become clear that *O* is radically incomplete, in view of the fact that this latter premise is clearly in need of defence.' But, with respect to *most* non-mathematical possibility claims (for example, 'It is possible that my name is Dore and that it will rain on 4 July in the year 2000'), there is no onus on their advocate to *prove* them; rather, the onus is on their critic to *disprove* them. And it is far from clear why anyone should think 'A supremely perfect being is logically possible' is an exception to this rule.

4.6 We are now in a position to reply to the objection of 1.6. I said in effect in 4.2 that it is obvious that a person who does *not* love kindness and hate cruelty is less perfect in that respect than a person who does. But *ex hypothesi* the SPB cannot be improved upon. Hence, he cannot love cruelty and hate kindness. So the premise in the 1.6 objection that it is possible that he does so is false. Moreover, the claim that it is possible for *human* IOs to love cruelty and hate kindness does not entail that it is possible that cruelty is good and kindness is bad, since the attitudes of the SPIO are in all instances canonical. And in any case it follows from my anti-sceptical argument in 4.3 that the SPIO would not permit such a divergence from his own attitudes with respect to human IOs, i.e. that argument shows that in fact it is *not* possible even for *human* IOs to love cruelty (greed, etc.) and hate kindness (honesty, etc.).

Here someone may say,

> It is no doubt true that an SPB, *qua* SPB, cannot hate kindness and love cruelty. But it is not possible for kindness to be bad and cruelty to be good only if it is not possible for the SPIO *not* to be an SPB. And why should we think that is not possible?

The answer is as follows. Argument *O* establishes that it is a necessary truth that an SPB exists. And necessary truths are true in all possible worlds. Hence, there is an SPB in all possible worlds. And, as we have seen, it is not possible for the SPB to be rivalled (4.4), i.e. there is no possible world in which the SPB of our world is rivalled. So either there is no SPB in other possible words or the SPB in those worlds is identical with the SPB in our world. But, again, there *is* an SPB in every possible world. So the SPB of our world, though he exists in all possible worlds, does not exist *qua non*-SPB in any of them, i.e. it is not possible for the (one and only) SPB *not* to be an SPB.

We can now address ourselves to a very common objection to theistic moral theories: namely, that they entail that, if God did not love kindness, then (*per impossibile*) it would not be good, *and*, if God did not hate cruelty, then (*per impossibile*) it would not be bad. The reply is that, since it is not possible that kindness is bad and cruelty is good, the antecedent of 'If God did not love kindness, then it would not be good' and the antecedent of 'If God did not hate cruelty, then it would not be bad' are necessary falsehoods, and it follows that the envisaged conditionals are vacuous, since a necessary falsehood entails *any* proposition, including the proposition that kindness *is* good and the proposition that cruelty *is* bad.

4.7 I have said that the reason why not all human beings are IOs is that it is better that we freely choose to be IOs than that God forces us to have the status. And this is reminiscent of Descartes's apparent claim that our mistakes, including our perceptual mistakes, are due to a misuse of our free will. It looks on occasion as if Descartes means to argue that, since God exists and is perfectly good, he would not permit us to be deceived about our perception of the external world, unless we freely deceive ourselves.

But, if one knows that the external world does in fact exist, then one knows that there are dreamers and madmen, about whom it is surely not always true that their dreams and hallucinations are blameworthy. And, if God will allow some people to be *always* deceived, through no fault of their own, and all human beings to be *sometimes* deceived when the deception is not merited, why should *I* think that I am not always dreaming or hallucinating? That is to say, why should I not argue as follows?

If many of my perceptions are non-delusory, then I know, at the very least, that people's perceptions are often delusory. Hence, if many of my perceptions are non-delusory, then I have reason to believe that this is *not*, in fact, the case. So either it is false that many of my perceptions are non-delusory or I have reason to believe that that is false. Hence, the second disjunct is true.

I do not mean to endorse this argument. Indeed, I have in effect argued elsewhere that it can be overcome.[4] I intend only to maintain (1) that it appears to be a serious stumbling-block for Descartes and (2) that *my* free-will defence is much more plausible than (on the envisaged common reading of Descartes) his is. For, though it is plain that dreamers and madmen normally violate neither moral nor epistemic obligations, it is far from clear that this is normally true of mistaken moralizers. Indeed, I am sure that almost everyone who has encountered non-qualified moral judges believes that they are violating epistemic obligations and that, if they are making judgements about weighty moral matters, then they are violating moral obligations as well.

But why does God bring it about that *some* human beings are *incapable* of being IOs, so that their mistaken moral judgements are not their own fault? The answer is that this question falls under the heading of the problem of evil, which has been discussed in Chapter 3 and will be discussed again in Chapter 5. Here I shall simply remark that it surely does not follow just from the fact that some people are retarded or criminally insane either that *no one* is an IO or that *no* human being is a free moral agent who has the ability freely to bring it about that he is an IO.

4.8 There is more to be said about moral knowledge. In particular, we need to examine the question of how human IOs who are not acquainted with the IOT and/or my justification of it can have justified moral beliefs. A brief answer is that, whether or not a person knows of the IOT and its justification, in fact his becoming an IO with respect to something, *X*, and discovering that he has a pro or con attitude toward *X*, is *a reliable method* for forming moral beliefs and, hence, he is justified in holding his belief about *X* if he uses that method.

The epistemologically sophisticated reader will recognize

here a version of externalist reliabilism, i.e. a version of the thesis that a person is justified in believing that p, if his belief that p is arrived at by a reliable method – by a method which generates true beliefs – whether or not he knows that the method is reliable. An argument for externalist reliabilism is that, for example, a child who sees his parents a few feet in front of him might well be justified in believing that his parents are nearby (whereas a child who merely imagined that his parents were nearby would not), even though he has no knowledge of the reliable process which gives rise to his belief and, since he has no concept of evidence, is not aware of evidence for his belief.[5]

The foregoing characterization of reliabilism is incomplete. Suppose that a person whose true belief that p is based on a reliable method, M, for causing beliefs of that sort has a good reason, of which he is aware, to believe that p is false and/or a good reason, of which he is aware, to believe falsely that M is *not* a reliable method. Then, though his true belief that p is arrived at by a reliable method, he is plainly unjustified in believing that p. Hence, we are in need of the following qualification:

> Someone, S, is justified in believing that p if (a) S's belief that p is produced by a reliable method, M, and (b) S neither has a good reason, of which he is aware, to believe that not-p, nor has a good reason, of which he is aware, to believe that M is not a reliable method, and (let us add for good measure) nothing of which he is aware is such that he epistemically *should* recognize it as such a reason.

This entails that not *all* justification can be accounted for solely in terms of reliable methods of which one need not be aware. For, needless to say, the externalist would be stated on an unacceptable regress were he to claim that the envisaged qualification need not be formulated in terms of evidence, of which one is aware, but can make do simply by referring to a reliable method. But this should be distressing only to those externalists who believe that *all* epistemology is reducible to empirical psychology.

4.9   Alvin Plantinga has recently raised this objection to reliabilism: 'A belief-forming process might be reliable, but only accidentally so, in which case the beliefs to which it gave rise would not be justified.'[6] By way of example, he asks us to imagine a case in which, due to cosmic radiation, someone forms a belief, about one of the first one thousand natural numbers, that it is not prime, whenever he hears the word 'prime' in any context. Naturally, most of those beliefs are true: the process is reliable. But the beliefs which it produces are surely not justified.

If we are inclined to accept Plantinga's criticism, it is, I think, because, given his example, *any* process at all, including guessing and playing hunches, would yield a roughly similar number of true beliefs. The process which he envisages is not so much *accidental* as it is *unnecessary*. Let us alter Plantinga's example, then, as follows: due to cosmic radiation, whenever a person hears the word 'prime' he forms mostly true beliefs about various aspects of particle physics, and the likelihood of his forming those beliefs by mere guessing or hunch-playing is enormously small. Here the reliabilist would not be remiss were he to stand his ground and maintain that the envisaged beliefs are in fact justified. In short, the reliabilist can fall back on the following, non-*ad hoc* qualification: 'One's belief is justified by a reliable method, *M*, only if the belief is not such that mere guessing or hunch-playing would yield true, closely similar beliefs roughly as often as *M* does.'

Another of Plantinga's counter-examples is this:

Consider . . . the person [who has a brain tumour which is] such that associated with it are a number of cognitive processes . . . most of which cause its victim to hold absurd beliefs. One of the processes associated with the tumor, however, causes the victim to believe that he has a brain tumor. . . . And suppose that [he] has no evidence at all for this belief . . . surely it is not true that this belief – the belief that he has a brain tumor – has much by way of positive epistemic status for [him].[7]

But in order to accommodate *this* counter-example the reliabilist need only add the following qualification:

> If an abnormal process in *S* gives rise to some of *S*'s beliefs, then, if and only if those beliefs are *mainly true, S* is justified in holding them (barring that *S* is aware of evidence against those beliefs or against the claim that the abnormal process is reliable).

4.10   My externalist approach to justified moral belief can be extended to belief in the existence of God. Historically, the vast majority of people in the West have believed truly that *X*'s being morally good or bad is roughly the same as God's favouring it or opposing it. So, since becoming an IO is a reliable method for forming the belief that *X* is morally good or bad, it is *eo ipso* a reliable method for forming the belief that God favours or disfavours *X* and *a fortiori* for forming the belief that God exists.

4.11   I have claimed that it is logically impossible to surpass, or even rival, God with respect to the number and degree of his perfections. Call this claim *C*. It looks as though it follows from *C* that, since being an IO is a perfection in God, all *human* IOs must be radically defective – so defective, indeed, that radical moral scepticism is, after all, correct.

However, my argument in 4.3 (that God would not permit widespread falsity in our moral judgements so long as we make an effort to be IOs) appears to be sound. Hence, it constrains us to qualify *C* as follows. There is a *prima facie* case, with respect to any perfection which varies in degree, for believing that God possesses it completely and, hence, that no other being can even approximate to possessing it completely. However, this *prima facie* case can be overridden *if the only alternative is that God lacks an even greater perfection*. And, if human beings could not emulate God with respect to the perfection of being an IO, then God would lack the even greater perfection of having created a world in which there are responsible moral agents.

The envisaged qualification does not affect the thesis that it is logically impossible to rival God with respect to the *number* of his perfections; and, of course, it does not affect the thesis that there are many perfections which God and other persons have in common (for instance, love), and which are such that the difference between God and others, with respect to the *degree* of those perfections, is enormous. Hence, even in view of the contemplated qualification of *C*, the central thesis of 4.4 – that argument *O* (of Chapter 2) does not commit us to a bloated ontology – remains unaffected.

4.12   Finally, we need to consider the following objection.

Dore's proof of the existence of God is, among other things, a proof of a perfectly morally good being. But Dore maintains that it is roughly true that the moral goodness of something *consists* in its being favoured by God. And the circular claim that the source of moral goodness is a morally good being casts no light at all on the nature of moral goodness. But in fact we can replace 'perfectly morally good', in the account of the nature of God, with 'maximally self-loving': the moral goodness of

God consists in *his loving himself*, just as a human's moral goodness consists of his being loved by God; and the *perfect* moral goodness of God consists of his loving himself so much that it is not logically possible for him to love himself more.

Here my objector may say,

> Whether or not Dore's account of the *nature of morality* is circular, the arguments of 4.2 and 4.3, taken together, constitute a circular *argument*. For 4.2 contains the moral judgement that God is perfectly good, and, hence, the rejection of moral scepticism in 4.3 presupposes what it tries to prove: namely, that some moral judgements are true.

My reply is that 'One of the attributes of a supremely perfect being would be perfect moral goodness' need not be taken as a piece of positive moral evaluation of God, i.e. it need not be taken to be a expression of a pro attitude on the part of the speaker. For that statement would be *true* even if made by Satan or by a moral nihilist. The reason for this is that the concept of perfection is a 'thick' concept like the concepts of, say, courage and generosity. Just as 'Jones is courageous but he always runs from even minor dangers' and 'Smith is generous, but he never helps family and friends when they are in need' would be clearly absurd, even in the mouth of a psychopath, so, too, 'He is a perfect person, but a thorough going moral scoundrel' would also be clearly absurd.

But is it equally clear that a perfectly morally good being would be, if a creator of persons, a creator of free moral agents about whose behaviour he could have pro attitudes? The answer is that we know that God exists (see Chapter 2) and that he has created people who appear to be free moral agents. Hence, we have a mix of empirical and non-empirical evidence that in fact God *has* created free moral agents, which in turn confirms the not *per se* implausible claim that a perfectly good and omnipotent being would, because of his goodness and power, do so.

Similar considerations apply to kindness and cruelty, about which I have been presupposing that we can know that a morally perfect being would normally love the one and hate the other. '*S* is a morally perfect being, though he hates all instances of kindness and loves all instances of cruelty', is, on the face of it, plainly absurd.

But what about the judgement that God *is* a perfect being? Is *that* not itself a moral judgement? The answer is that the sentence 'God is a perfect being' expresses a definition, and, hence, does not belong to the class of *bona fide* moral judgements. A proof of this is that, if Satan were to say, 'Contrary to popular opinion, God is an imperfect being', we would accuse him not of being morally perverse, but rather of having language problems. (Satan might, of course, say with linguistic propriety, but moral perversity, 'God is a perfect being, and that is a despicable way to be', even if he were an IO, since it is at least *possible* that there are conflicting IO intuitions.)

5 The Problem of Moral Evil

5.1 I have said that God, a supremely perfect being, would have appropriate pro and con attitudes toward human beings and their actions. But here someone may ask, 'Why would God have any *con* attitudes? No doubt he *does*, if he exists, have con attitudes toward wrongdoers, *since they exist*. But why does he permit them to exist?' The reader will recognize in this question the basis of the atheistic argument from moral evil. In much of what follows, I shall be discussing the question of whether that argument can be refuted in terms of the question of whether the best candidate for refuting it – the so-called 'free-will defence' – is sound.

5.2 Alvin Plantinga's famous version of the free-will defence[1] can be formulated as follows:

> One of God's perfections is his having created other persons. And it is better that these persons should be free moral agents, rather than innocent automata. But, since freely doing what is right requires an ability to do otherwise, free moral agents must have a capacity for wrongdoing. Moreover, it is logically impossible for God to *cause* someone to refrain from wrongdoing while allowing him to do so freely. Hence, even though he is omnipotent, it is not in God's power to prevent the harm which is done by free moral wrongdoers. And, since the positive value of free right choices outweighs the negative value of harmful wrong choices, and, since we free moral agents frequently freely choose to do what is right, God is justified in permitting the harm which we do.

An obvious objection to this defence is that, since there is an indefinitely large number of sets of person-properties, it must be that the instantiations of *some* of those sets would, though they had a capacity for wrongdoing, never in fact exercise it. But Plantinga replies that it may be, for all the atheist can prove to the contrary, that it is a brute (and unhappy) fact that any possible world which contains an acceptable balance of good free choices over wrong free choices is one in which all, or many, of any given set of instantiations of person-properties will sometimes exercise their capacity for wrongdoing. In Plantinga's terminology, the atheist cannot show that it is false that all (personal) creaturely essences suffer from 'transworld depravity'.[2]

But is not the doctrine of transworld depravity obviously implausible, in view of the indefinitely large number of person-essences which God had to choose from? J. L. Mackie writes as follows about this:

> How is it possible that every creaturely essence suffers from transworld depravity? This possibility would be realized only if God were faced with a limited range of creaturely essences, a limited number of possible people from which he had to make a selection, if he was to create free agents at all. What can be supposed to have presented him with that limited range?[3]

What Mackie says here is not so much a reasoned refutation of Plantinga as rather a claim that the doctrine of transworld depravity is obviously implausible. I shall return to a discussion of this matter later in the chapter.

5.3   There is another objection to the free-will defence.

The free-will defence essentially involves the mistaken claim that, if a person's actions have causes, then they are *ipso facto* not freely performed. If we abandon this claim, as we should, then there will be no obstacle to our seeing that God could have created the world in such a way that every free mortal agent was causally guaranteed to do only what is right.

Antony Flew has used roughly the following paradigm-case argument[4] against the claim that free will and causation are incompatible (the incompatibility thesis).

We are taught the meaning of 'freely chosen' and 'freely done' by being referred to cases in which a person does, or can do, what he chooses to do. And these are perfectly compatible with his choices and actions having causes. Contra-causal freedom is simply the product of muddled metaphysics.

But is it really the case that ordinary language-users are not incompatibilists? Suppose (what is logically possible) that it were discovered that all our choices and actions were the result of the post-hypnotic suggestions of a Great Hypnotist. Or suppose that I discovered that all my choices and actions came about as the result of an evil scientist who is controlling my experiences, beliefs, choices and actions by means of a diabolical brain-machine. Surely I should not be justified in these cases in maintaining that, in view of the paradigm-case argument, I had been acting and choosing freely all along.

Everyone agrees that certain *kinds* of causes are incompatible with our choosing and acting freely. Actions produced by a hypnotist or by neurotic compulsion are examples. But I know of no plausible explanation of why these causes should be incompatible with free choice and actions while most other causes are not. Mackie says that free choices and actions are those which follow from one's nature, and that, since one's nature has a causal history, so have one's free choices and actions.[5] But this of no help, unless it is made

Moral Scepticism

clear why, say, acting from neurotic compulsion, or because of the brain states brought about by a hypnotist, does *not* count as 'acting from one's nature'. It will not do to say here that, in the envisaged cases, one is choosing and acting against one's desire: I might be glad to do what I am made to do by a hypnotist or what I am neurotically compelled to do (for instance, steal watches), so long as my behaviour does not get me into trouble.

Finally, I think that the following simple argument shows that determinism is not compatible with free choices and actions. I choose and act freely only if my choices and actions are not brought about by causes over which I have no control. Thus, if an action of mine *in present time* has a certain sufficient causal condition, the existence or operation of which I am powerless to prevent, then I do not perform that action freely. But, if determinism (on the macroscopic level) is correct, then any choice and action of mine is the end product of a causal series which stretches back to *a time long before I was born* and *a fortiori* to a time when I had no control over events which would turn out to be causally sufficient for those choices and actions.

But, now, if free choice is incompatible with natural causation of the kind envisaged, then anyone who claims that it *is* compatible with God's causation owes us an explanation of why that should be so. And I know of no philosopher who has attempted to formulate such an explanation.

5.4 Though we have just examined the question of whether free will and determinism are compatible, we have yet to discuss the question of whether human beings do *in fact* have free will. Now, it may appear as though they do not. For consider the following argument.

If someone, *S*, is contra-causally free, then he has it in his power to violate true, law-like propositions. Consider the true, law-like proposition (for simplicity, 'the causal law') 'If X, then not-B', where this means 'If X obtains, then S does not exhibit bodily motion B.' And suppose that X obtains. Now consider a free choice, C, such that the following is a true, law-like proposition: 'If S makes choice C, then bodily motion B results.' *Ex hypothesi* there are no causal constraints on S's making choice C. So, since *ex hypothesi* X obtains, and it is causally possible for S to make choice C, it is causally possible for S to violate a causal law.

One reply to this argument is as follows.

There can be no such thing as the violation of a *bona fide* causal law, only the *falsification* of a *putative* causal law. (This is reminiscent of a well-known critique of the concept of a miracle.) So, *if*, in fact, S makes choice C and X obtains, 'If X, then not-B' is not after all a causal law.

But this reply is unacceptable, for surely S (a human person) does not have it in his power to falsify putative causal laws at will.

Let us try again, then. Suppose that, instead of saying that, when S-like people make C-like choices, they violate causal laws like 'If X, then not-B' (or falsify putative laws of that kind), one maintains that, whenever S-like people make C-like choices, X-like states of affairs do not obtain. The obvious objection to this move is that it is highly implausible that it is a mere coincidence that X-like states of affairs never obtain then. And, of course, it is. But, as we have seen, it is likely that God exists (*pace* the argument from suffering) and also likely that deterministic compatibilism is false; so it is open to the free-will defender to fall back on the claim that God brings it about that X-like states of affairs never obtain on the occasions which we are contemplating. (This does not involve law-violation at a higher level, if God deals with, for example, 'If Z then X' in a similar manner.)

5.5   There is an ancient argument for fatalism which, since it is *eo ipso* an argument against free will, merits our attention here.

> Suppose that at a given moment, M_2, I do not perform a certain action, A. Then, at any given previous moment, M_1, the sentence 'I shall not perform A at M_2' expressed a true proposition. But, if I were able to perform A at M_2, then I should be able to render it *false* that the envisaged sentence expressed a true proposition, i.e. I should be able to change the past. And I am surely not able to do that. Hence, for any action which I do not perform at a given moment, M, I am unable to perform that action at M, i.e. I do not have it in my power to do what in fact I do not do. So I do not have free will.

This argument is a remarkably simple one, in view of its weighty conclusion. But there is any equally simple reply. My having it in my power to do A at M_2, even though at M_1 'I shall not do A at M_2' expressed a true proposition, entails that, *if* at M_1 I had been going to choose to do A at M_2, *then* the sentence 'I shall not do A at M_2' would *not* have expressed a true proposition at M_1. But this conditional proposition (call it q) is perfectly compatible with my being unable to change the past. And, if p ('I have it in my power to do A at M_2, even though at M_1 "I shall not do A at M_2" expressed a true proposition') entails q, and not-w ('I am not able to change the past') is logically compatible with q, then p is logically compatible with not-w. (If every possible p world is a q world, and there is a possible world in which p and, hence, q are true, and in which not-w is also true, then *a fortiori* not every p-world is a w-world.) It follows that 'I have it in my power to do A at M_2, even though at M_1 "I shall not do A at M_2" expressed a true proposition' does *not* entail the absurd conclusion that I am able to change the past.

The reader may recall G. E. Moore's compatibilist analysis of being able to do otherwise, which touched off many years of discussion of ifs and cans. It goes roughly as follows.

'I am able to do other than what I did do at a given moment, *M*' means that (1) I *would* have done other than I did do at M *if* I had chosen to do so, and (2) I was able at *M* to choose to do so.

But the analysis is unacceptable. If we omit (2), then we have the distressing consequence that I was able to do other than what I did at *M*, even though a drug or a hypnotist caused me to be unable to choose to do so. For the latter is perfectly compatible with my being such that I *would* have done other than I did do *if* I had so chosen. However, adding 'and I was *able* so to choose' does not really improve matters, since the envisaged locution is, if Moore is right about ifs and cans, itself subject to the contemplated analysis, and so on *ad infinitum*. (A defender of Moore might wish to claim that 'able' in 'I was able to choose' does not have the same meaning as 'able' in, for example, 'I was able to run a six-minute mile.' But then we are owed a clarification of the meaning of this alleged homonym.)

Does the failure of Moore's version of ifs and cans entail that we ought to reject my critique of fatalism as well? The answer is 'No.' The trouble with Moorean attempts to defend compatibilism with respect to free will is that, if, as Mooreans believe, determinism (on the macroscopic level) is really true, then the anecedents of Moorean conditionals are nomically false, i.e. it is always causally impossible to satisfy the descriptions contained in the if clause. But the anti-fatalist is not (or, at any rate, should not be) a determinist.

He holds (or should hold) that the antecedent of '*If* I had been going to choose to do A at M_2, *then* "I shall not do it at M_2", spoken at M_1, would *not* have expressed a true proposition' does not contain a description of me which it is causally impossible for me to satisfy.

Thus far I have formulated fatalism in terms of 'I shall not do A at M_2' expressing a true proposition at M_1. But, of course, fatalism can be – and historically most often has been – formulated in terms of the thesis that God *knows* at M_1 that 'I shall not do A at M_2' expresses a true proposition. Indeed, it has been frequently overlooked that God's knowing this is not a prerequisite of fatalism *per se*. Fatalism is no less plausible when it is formulated *just* in terms of 'I shall not do A at M_2' expressing a true proposition at M_2, without reference to God's *knowing* at M_1 that the quoted sentence is true. Moreover, fatalism can be just as cogently formulated in terms of *anyone's* knowing at M_1 that I shall not do A at M_2.

But, in any case, what we can call '*cognitive* fatalism' can be rejected for a reason which is similar to my reason for rejecting non-cognitive fatalism. To say that I have it in my power to do A at M_2, even though at M_1 someone (for example, God) knew that I would not do A at M_2, is to express a proposition which entails '*If* I had been going to do A at M_2, *then* he would *not* have known at M_1 that "I shall not do A at M_2" expressed a true proposition.' So long as the antecedent of this counterfactual is not nomically false, this is a perfectly acceptable explication of my having it in my power to do A at M_2, even when someone knows at M_1 that I shall not do A at M_2.

5.6 Let us now consider another objection to Plantinga.

Plantinga's central thesis is that it may well be that even an omnipotent being could not instantiate a creaturely essence which contains the property 'always freely does what is right'.[6] Now, suppose that by 'always freely does what is right' Plantinga means 'freely avoids doing wrong on all (specifiable) occasions'. Then God's causing a person to refrain from doing wrong on a given occasion necessitates his not instantiating a perfect person-essence, P, because (1) then P would have the property 'caused to avoid wrongdoing on at least one occasion' and (2) this is incompatible with his having the property 'freely avoids wrongdoing on *all* occasions'. But why should we be asked to assume that God wishes to instantiate person-essences who will freely avoid evil on all occasions? The fact that God has made us, for example, susceptible to being rendered unconscious against our will appears to indicate that it is not his aim to instantiate P-like essences. And, at any rate, Plantinga should have explicitly considered the possibility of God's instantiating a free and perfect person-essence, somewhat different from P, and, in this connection, the following objection to the free-will defence.

Let us call by the letter X the property of being such that there are *some* occasions on which one has a capacity for wrongdoing and no occasions on which one in fact does wrong. Since having X involves not doing wrong on occasions on which one is able to do wrong, it involves sometimes freely refraining from wrongdoing. Now let us consider a person-essence, Q, who possesses X. Q is unlike P in the following respect: God can, on *some* occasions, prevent the instantiation of Q (call him Jones) from performing wrong actions, thereby destroying Jones's capacity for wrongdoing (and, hence, his ability freely to shun wrongdoing) on those occasions. All that is necessary in order for Jones to be the instantiation of Q is that (1) there are *some* occasions on which Jones is able to do wrong and (2) Jones avoids wrongdoing on those occasions as well as all others.

Now let us ask why God does not instantiate person-essences who possess X. Shall we say that God's causing Jones to have X would necessarily be the same as God's causing Jones to avoid wrongdoing on all occasions, including even those on which Jones has a capacity for wrongdoing and, hence, is *not* caused by God to avoid wrongdoing? If we are entitled to say this, then of course we need not be tempted to attribute to God the power to see to it that Q is instantiated. We can say instead that, though God can *begin* the job of instantiating Q (by instantiating all of Jones's person-properties except X), it is up to Jones to complete the job by himself seeing to it that he comes to possess X.

But in fact God's causing Jones to possess X is plainly *not* necessarily the same as God's causing Jones to avoid wrongdoing on all those occasions when in fact Jones does so. Suppose that there are *some* occasions – call them O occasions – on which (1) Jones avoids wrongdoing and (2) neither God nor anyone but Jones is a cause of Jones's doing so. It is consistent to say that God could have caused Jones to possess X by simply preventing Jones from doing wrong on any *other* occasion. No doubt by so doing God would have brought it about that there would be some occasions on which Jones would be incapable of wrongdoing. So Jones would not have represented a free instantiation of Plantinga's P. But none the less he *would* have been the instantiation of a *kind* of perfect person-essence and one who is certainly preferable to the wrong-doers whom God, if he exists, has actually created. Hence, if God exists, then he can be faulted for not instantiating Q and other such person-essences.

Now, this apparently formidable objection can be met, though in a way which takes us beyond Plantinga. Either O occasions are such that God would have intervened on those occasions to prevent Jones from doing wrong, had he foreseen (what is contrary to fact) that Jones would do wrong on those occasions, barring God's intervention, or God would not have intervened. Suppose, first, that God would have intervened on those occasions. Then, even though O occasions are ones on which no one but Jones causes Jones to shun wrongdoing, O occasions would none the less *not* be occasions on which Jones has a capacity for wrongdoing. If it is true that an omnipotent being would have intervened to prevent Jones from doing wrong on some given occasion, O_1, had it been the case that otherwise Jones *would* have done wrong on O_1, then Jones had no real option with respect to wrongdoing on O_1: he could not have done other than avoid it. Hence, Jones would not *freely* have avoided wrongdoing on O_1. And what is true of O_1 is, of course, true of any other, similar occasions. It follows that the alternative now under discussion is not compatible with its being the case that *any* O occasions are ones on which Jones *freely* avoids wrongdoing. But *ex hypothesi* other occasions on which Jones avoids wrongdoing are (because of God's intervention on those occasions) also not ones on which he does so freely. So, given that the envisaged alternative obtained, Jones would not possess X and, hence, would not after all be the instantiation of Q. (Let us use 'Jones' not to refer to the instantiation of Q, but rather to refer to somebody having all of the properties, including individuating properties, which the instantiation of Q would have, except for the property of freely avoiding wrongdoing on any occasions when he has a capacity for wrongdoing.)

Suppose, then, that O occasions are such that, had Jones been going to engage in wrongdoing on those occasions, barring God's intervention, God would *not* have intervened to prevent Jones from going morally astray. And suppose (something to which the free-will defender will want to assent) that God is morally justified in not being disposed to intervene in the envisaged manner because, if he were thus disposed, Jones' acts of avoiding wrongdoing on O occasions would not be freely done. Then, given that Jones in fact does wrong on some occasions and, hence, turns out not to be the instantiation of Q, we are not warranted in maintaining that God is reprehensible for not preventing Jones from doing wrong (for not instantiating Q). If we grant (what is not now in dispute) that God *would* not have been reprehensible for permitting Jones to do wrong on occasions when in fact Jones shuns wrongdoing, then we cannot rationally claim that God *is* reprehensible for permitting Jones to do wrong on those occasions when in fact Jones goes morally astray. Plainly, we are not entitled to say, 'S would not have been reprehensible for performing an action, bearing a certain description, D, yesterday, but he is reprehensible for performing an action bearing description D today, even though there is no morally relevant difference between the action which S would not have been reprehensible for performing yesterday and the action which he is reprehensible for performing today.' And there is no morally relevant difference between the actions which God *would* have performed on O occasions when Jones freely shuns wrongdoing, *had* Jones been going to engage in wrongdoing (i.e. actions of permitting Jones to do what is wrong), and the actions which God *does* perform on occasions when in fact Jones *does* engage in wrongdoing (i.e. also actions of permitting Jones to go morally astray). Clearly it will not do to cite as a relevant difference here the fact that the latter actions are actual and the former are merely hypothetical (actions which God would have performed if . . . , but which he did not in fact perform). It is obviously preposterous to maintain that it follows just from the premise that a person did not in fact perform a certain action that he would not have been reprehensible for performing the action if he had in fact performed it.

The upshot is that, though Plantinga's answer to the question of why God does not instantiate only perfect person-essence is not, as it stands, complete, it can be supplemented by the foregoing justification of God for not instantiating only *Q*-like people.

5.7 We have seen that Plantinga's solution of the problem of why God does not instantiate only perfect person-essences needs to be supplemented by my own. But now it is time to point out that the theist can dispense with Plantinga's solution altogether.

There is a reason, other than Plantinga's, for rejecting the conclusion that God is morally reprehensible for failing to instantiate *P*-like person-essences. My solution of the problem of why God does not instantiate *Q*-like person-essences applies equally well to the problem of why God does not instantiate only *P*-like person-essences. Since those person-essences are free as well as perfect, it must be that God *would* have instantiated them even if (contrary to fact) they had been going to engage in wrongdoing. (In this case they would not have been the instantiations of perfect person-essences. 'Their instantiations' is here being used to refer to people having all of the properties – including individuating properties – of *P*-like essences, except for the property of never doing what is wrong.) And there is no morally relevant difference between the actions which God *would* have performed, if those instantiations had been going to do wrong (i.e. actions of instantiating them anyway), and God's actual actions of permitting the people whom he in fact creates to go morally astray. Now, God would have been justified in performing the former actions. Hence it must be false that he is reprehensible for performing the latter ones.

An argument for my claim that God would have permitted the envisaged instantiations to engage in wrongdoing if (contrary to fact) they had so chosen, is as follows.

Consider a given perfect person-essence, *P*. 'If the instantiation of *P* (call him "Smith") had been going to do something wrong on a given occasion, O, then P would not have been instantiated' entails 'If Smith had been going to do wrong on O, then he would not have existed then.' And it is plainly false that a person can be able to do something such that, had he been going to do it, then he would not have existed: existence is a necessary condition of a person's performing any action and *a fortiori* it is a necessary condition of a person's *having it in his power* to perform any action. It follows that 'Smith had it in his power to do wrong on O, though, if he had been going to do wrong on O, he would not have existed then' is no more acceptable than, say, 'Smith had it in his power to swim on O, even though, if he swam on O, there would have been no liquid in his vicinity then.'

The foregoing does not, of course, entail that God could not have actualized person-essences which would in fact, if actualized, have freely performed actions of refraining from wrongdoing and would never have performed any wrong actions. Hence, Mackie's quoted criticism of Plantinga does not apply here. But, given that the free-will defender is right in asserting that a world in which God's creatures frequently freely avoid wrongdoing is better than any world in which there is no free avoidance of wrongdoing, the foregoing does show that God would have been morally justified in *not* being disposed to prevent the wrongdoing of perfect person-instantiations if (contrary to fact) he foresaw that they would sometimes do wrong. And that is enough to support the claim that God is not reprehensible for permitting the wrongdoing of the instantiations of the person-essences whom he in fact instantiates. For there is no morally relevant difference between God's being disposed to permit (what is contrary to fact) wrongdoing on the part of perfect-person instantiations and his being disposed to permit the wrongdoing in which his non-perfect creatures in fact engage.

Finally, there is still another (related, non-Plantingan)

solution of the problem of how God can be justified in creating wrongdoers. I have pointed out that God cannot both instantiate Q (who freely avoids wrongdoing on O occasions) and be disposed to prevent Jones from doing wrong on O occasions, in the event of his foreseeing (what is contrary to fact) that otherwise Jones would do wrong then. Now it is time to point out that, for similar reasons, God cannot instantiate person-essences whose instantiations will be morally impeccable (either P-like instantiations or Q-like instantiations) and be disposed to instantiate *only* such essences. For God obviously has it in his power to fail to instantiate any person-essence who, if instantiated, would engage in wrongdoing. And, if he were disposed to *exercise* that power, then existence, a necessary condition of anyone's performing an action, and *a fortiori* a wrong action, would be missing. And that is incompatible with anyone's being a free moral agent and, indeed, with his being anything at all.

Once again, the foregoing does not entail that God could not have instantiated person-essences who, once instantiated, would always shun wrongdoing. So Mackie's quoted objection to Plantinga is also irrelevant to the present version of the free-will defence. What the foregoing *does* entail, however, is that, if free-will defenders are right in maintaining that a world in which God's creatures frequently freely avoid wrongdoing is better than any world which lacks that property, then God is morally justified, with respect to any person-essence – regardless of whether its instantiation will be morally blemished or not – in *not* being disposed to fail to instantiate it on the ground that its instantiation will be a wrongdoer.

5.8 I have said in effect that God cannot be faulted for permitting actual morally wrong choices, since he cannot be blamed for not being *disposed* to prevent wrong choices which are not in fact made but which someone has a capacity for making. 'But', my critic may say, this argument surely 'proves' too much. For it 'proves' that God would not have been reprehensible for instantiating only person-essences who made morally wrong choices but never morally *right* ones, despite having a *capacity* for making the latter choices. Dore is committed to this conclusion by his claim that, if God would not be reprehensible for not being disposed to prevent wrong choices which are not in fact made, then he is not reprehensible for not preventing wrong choices which *are* in fact made. For this claim (call it L) does not entail that there is a certain *percentage* of right choices in the total number of free choices, right and wrong: L is perfectly compatible with there being no such percentage at all.

One answer to this objection is that in fact L does imply that the percentage of morally right choices in the total number of free choices is greater than zero. For, in order to get a foothold, my argument must countenance cases in which, *though there is a freely chosen right action*, God would not have prevented its morally wrong counterpart if, contrary to fact, it were going to occur. My argument is that since – and *only* since – God is obviously *not* reprehensible for lacking the contemplated disposition in *that* kind of case, he is not reprehensible for failing to prevent free wrongdoing when in fact it occurs.

But why need it be true that there are more than *one*, or a very few, cases in which freely chosen right actions occur? Admittedly, *L per se* does not entail an answer to *that* question. But we have only to supplement L with the further claim that there *is* a morally relevant difference between God's not being disposed to intervene in a world in which there is an enormous balance of freely chosen wrong actions over freely chosen right actions, and his not being disposed to intervene in a world in which this is not the case.

But *precisely what* percentage of freely chosen right actions in the total number of free choices must there be in order for the 'no relevant difference' description to apply?

The answer is that the free-will defender need not answer *that* question. It is enough for him simply to affirm that the percentage is not negligible.

Still, the question does give rise to another objection:

Call the envisaged percentage (whatever it may be) P. Now, *ex hypothesi* God would not permit the percentage of free right actions to fall below P. So no given moral agent, M_1, has a capacity for bringing the level of free wrong actions to the point where the percentage of free right actions falls below P. Let us call a candidate for such a P-violating action A_1. Since *ex hypothesi* God would prevent A_1 from occurring, M_1 could not *freely refrain* from violating P. And exactly *similar* considerations apply to A_2 (the *next* potentially P-violating action from which M_1 should freely refrain), A_3 and so on, until we arrive at the conclusion that M_1's putative capacity of freely refraining from wrongdoing is in fact non-existent.

My reply is that, since we know that God exists (via argument O), and since there appears to be a strong likelihood that the free-will defence is the correct solution to the problem of moral evil, we should conclude that, if M_1 were freely to engage in what otherwise would be a P-violating action, then *other* moral agents would freely perform *P-restoring* actions. But this reply is in need of elaboration.

Consider a given moral agent, M_2, who freely performs a P-restoring action. If M_2 had *refrained* from doing so, then he would in effect have freely performed a *P-violating* action. So it looks as though the same slippery-slope argument that appeared to establish that M_1 is not a free moral agent applies also to M_2. And, indeed, this is the case if, in considering P-restoring moral agents, we arrive at a point where there are no further compensating moral agents. What is indicated, then, is the positing of an *indefinitely large number* of compensating moral agents. This move would, of course, be wildly *ad hoc* if we did not have a reason to believe that God exists and would want some of his creatures to be free moral agents. But in fact we do have reason to believe this.

5.9 In his well-known article 'Middle Knowledge and the Problem of Evil'[7] Robert Merrihew Adams argues that it is false 'that God knows with certainty what every possible free creature would freely do in every situation in which the creature could possibly find himself . . . on the ground that conditional propositions [of the form "If, contrary to fact, Smith had found himself in circumstances *C*, then he would freely have chosen to do *A*"] cannot be true'.[8] I shall not discuss Adams's argument further here. For, even if he is right, it is demonstrable that the free-will defender does not *require* the thesis that God has the envisaged kind of knowledge. Since God would not have refrained from actualizing a set of person-properties if (contrary to fact) he had foreseen that its actualization would go morally astray in a given set of circumstances, God *need* not have known what the instantiations of any given set of person-properties would do in any given set of circumstances in which he might place them, and *a fortiori* he need not have known what *contrary to fact* they *would* have done in a given set of circumstances in which he did not in fact place them. All that God needs to know is (1) that there is an indefinitely large number of free moral agents and (2) that a sufficiently large percentage of them will not engage in wrongdoing to the extent that the percentage of morally good actions which they perform falls below *P*. And, since he knows all that it is logically possible for him to know, then, if Adams is right, the presently envisaged knowledge does not entail his knowing, of individual sets of person-properties, what they would have done if, contrary to fact, he had placed them in such and such a set of circumstances.

5.10 The free-will defender needs to answer the following question:

> Given that the value of free virtuous choices and actions is sufficiently great to outweigh the negative value of immoral, harmful choices and actions, why should it be the case that, with respect to human beings, it is frequently morally admissible – and, indeed, obligatory – to restrain people from doing great harm? If God forbears to intervene against serious wrongdoers, how can it be right for human beings to do so?

The answer is simply that, if God, an omnipotent being, *always* prevented harmful choices and actions, then he would totally abolish free will. And, of course, human beings, unlike God, can prevent only a limited number of harmful actions, and so do not have the power to destroy human freely chosen actions altogether. But why cannot God be faulted for not at least preventing those very freely chosen actions which it is not wrong for *human beings* to prevent? The answer is that there is no morally relevant difference between God's failure to prevent just *those* instances of wrongdoing and his failure to prevent *other* instances of wrongdoing. And, since, if the free-will defender is right, God is not reprehensible for his failure to prevent the latter instances, he is not blameworthy for failing to prevent the former instances as well, given that free will really is sufficiently valuable to outweigh the negative value of the harm which results from our having it.

But can it really be the case that God can be justified in permitting the enormous harm which, say, *Hitler* did? The answer is (1) that there is no morally relevant difference between God's failure to prevent the harm which billions of *ordinary* wrongdoers do and his failure to prevent the harm which is done by such monstrous individuals as Hitler, and

(2) that we have no reason to believe that God should considerably reduce the number of moral agents who inhabit the universe, since we have no reason to believe that his doing so would not substantially diminish the percentage of free right actions in the total number of free actions, right and wrong.

5.11 If we are to suppose that the free-will defence accounts adequately for the fact that the SPIO (God) has con attitudes, as well as pro attitudes, toward created moral agents, then we must view it as an adequate solution of the problem of moral evil. And, as such, it provides the theist with at least a partial answer to the question 'Why does God permit suffering?', since a good deal of suffering is the result of wrongful behaviour. Now, Plantinga has suggested that the theist can extend the free-will defence to *non-human* moral agents and in *that* way provide himself with theistic account of *all* suffering.[9]

I think that, in the absence of reason to believe that God exists, this move would be unacceptably *ad hoc*. And, even given the plausibility of argument *O* (or some other evidence for God's existence, if such there be), we are here confronted with a question which is similar to one which I raised in Chapter 3: namely, the question of whether the evidence for God's existence, when coupled with defences against the atheistic argument from suffering in which extra-empirical entities (in the present case, extra-empirical moral agents) play a role, is sufficiently strong to outweigh the force of the latter argument.

But the Chapter 3 answer applies here: there is a *prima facie* case against moral scepticism which tilts the balance in favour of theism. Moreover, given the plausibility of the free-will defence, the theist can feel more comfortable about the argument from suffering than if his only way of coping with it is the way which I discussed in Chapter 3. For the chance that *neither* solution is sufficiently plausible to justify us in thinking that argument *O* is not overridden by the argument from suffering is greater than the chance that just *one* of those solutions is that plausible.

Or is it? In two prior works[10] I have argued against the thesis that overcoming a capacity for wrongdoing is sufficiently valuable to justify God in permitting us to have such a capacity, on the grounds that (1) a person can have a capacity for, for example, raping children only if he is sometimes *inclined* to rape children, and (2), even though he did not give in to this inclination, his sometimes having it would be a profound character defect, rather than something that made him better off.

However, I now think that (2) may well be false. In Chapter 6 I shall argue in effect that an individual's being inclined to do what is evil constitutes a defect only if it gives rise to desire-frustration. If this is correct, then having a capacity for raping children is not a defect in a person who will never exercise it. I submit that, if we think otherwise, this is because we know that such an individual is *statistically* much more likely to rape children than are normal people. But mere statistics do not constitute moral defectiveness.

5.12 In any case, even if extending the free-will defence, in terms of extra-empirical moral agents, were unacceptably *ad hoc*, it remains true that, since compatibilism with respect to free will is mistaken, and since it is deeply embedded in common sense that many human beings are on occasion able to do other than what they in fact do when they inflict suffering, common sense commits us to the conclusion that it is false that *all* suffering is entailed by *S* (see 3.1), i.e. it is false, given common sense, that there is a true, law-like statement 'If *C*, a free choice or the result of a free choice, occurs, then *Z* suffers' which is such that its antecedent is entailed by *S*. *C* is entailed by *S* only if *C* could not have failed to occur, given S; and, since C is a free choice or the result of a free choice, this is not the case. It follows that, if common sense is right, then my Chapter 3 solution of the problem of suffering is not true of the suffering which results from moral evil, whatever may be thought of the claim that it is true of suffering which does not. But we can cope with that fact simply by adding that what is logically necessary for the valuable end of 3.1 is not just S, but *S plus the free choices of human moral agents*.

5.13   Finally, we need to consider the following objection.

> Argument O of Chapter 2 establishes that it is a conceptual truth that God exists. But conceptual truths are *necessary* truths, i.e. it is necessarily false that God, a supremely perfect being, does not exist. And a necessary condition of being supremely perfect is never doing what is morally evil. So it is a necessary truth that God never engages in morally unacceptable behaviour. It follows that God has no capacity for wrongdoing and, hence, is not a free moral agent. How, then, can it be a good thing that human beings and other created moral agents are endowed with free will?

The most plausible reply to this objection is that it is a perfection in God that he is morally causally self-sufficient, i.e. that his morally significant actions are entirely determined by his own nature. However, if created moral agents were not to some extent contra-causally free, then all of our actions would be caused by external factors over which we have no control. And free will is only a perfection in a rational being whose putatively morally significant actions would be entirely determined by the Big Bang or some such external phenomenon were he not to some extent contra-causally free. But, again, God does *not* fit that description:

none of his morally significant actions are determined by things other than himself, and, hence, free moral agency, which necessarily involves a capacity for wrongdoing, would not be a perfection in God.

But why did God not bestow causal self-sufficiency on his human creatures? The question is self-answering. It is logically impossible for an external being to *cause* us to be causally self-sufficient. But why did the supremely perfect being not cause us to be causally self-sufficient, *except* for his causing us to be such that *from then on* all of our morally significant actions would be determined by our own natures? The answer is that it is evidently logically impossible for us to rival God with respect to the perfection of being causally self-sufficient. (Let me remind the reader that there is a strong *prima facie* case, with respect to *any* perfection of God, for the claim that it is not logically possible for anyone else to rival him with respect to it. And the thesis that this is true of causal self-sufficiency is strengthened by the consideration that in fact human beings do *not* possess that perfection.)

6 Desire-Utilitarianism

6.1   We have seen that scepticism with respect to attitude theories in general, which entails the distressing consequence that moral utterances are all false, can be overcome. But there is another less severe kind of scepticism which philosophical laymen would not find as distressing as do or would professional moralists: namely, scepticism about whether it is possible to devise an adequate theory which possesses what John Rawls calls 'wide reflective equilibrium', i.e. which explains and predicts the intuitions (attitudes) of IOs and, to some extent, enables us to correct borderline intuitions. We now know that some things are morally good and some things are morally bad and that these are things which are (and would be) favoured, in the case of morally good things, and disfavoured, in the case of morally bad things, by an IO; but we also need a general account of precisely what those things are or should be.

6.2   It will be useful to begin the search for such a theory by using as a touchstone for any explanation of IO intuitions the following two:

1   There is a *prima facie* case on behalf of not killing young children, even when no adults can be found who want to raise them.
2   Opposition to artificial contraception is ill-founded.

In what follows, I shall argue that what I shall call 'desire-utilitarianism' – the theory that what is, in general, morally good is the satisfaction of the desires of sentient beings, and what is, in general, morally bad is the frustration of those desires – gives us the best account of these intuitions and of other IO intuitions.

73

But first I should say something about the claim, made by conservative Roman Catholics, that the use of artificial contraceptives is 'unnatural' and, hence, wrong. If 'unnatural' is being used here simply to mean 'wrong', then of course the assertion is circular; and if it is being used to mean 'infrequent', as in 'This is not the grizzly bear's natural habitat', and 'It not natural for people to keep their eyes closed when they are not drowsy', then it is plainly false (at least in countries with a large middle class) and, anyway, has nothing to do with morality. But the only alternative is that it is being used as a pseudo-technical term, i.e. as a term which is not being used in its normal sense, but which has not been assigned any clear alternative meaning. (That conservative Roman Catholics are thoroughly confused about the matter – and hence far from being IOs – is borne out by the fact that, though they evidently think that the use of, say, the birth-control pill is not an instance of merely omitting to get pregnant, they also think that the use of the so-called 'rhythm method' is such an instance, even though it involves the dutiful keeping of charts and taking of temperatures and the clear intention to avoid pregnancy.)

6.3 Kantianism, contractarianism (of which the most notable recent defender is John Rawls), communitarianism (the theory that morality has to do with societal roles), classical utilitarianism (the theory that what is, in general, morally good is that which increases pleasure and what is, in general, morally bad is that which decreases it and causes pain) and desire-utilitarianism are nowadays the academic moral theories which are most frequently discussed, and I shall assume that, if scepticism is to be avoided, then at least one of them can be seen to be correct. But it follows from the *prima facie* case against killing young children (intuition 1) that contractarianism and Kantianism are false. Both Kantianism and contractarianism essentially involve the claim that each of us should and, for the most part do, respect the interests only of other beings who are capable of respecting our interests. And young children do not in fact satisfy this description. Moreover, since (very) young children normally do not play roles in the extra-familial community, communitarianism entails that they have no moral status; it cannot, therefore, account for the *prima facie* case against killing them, even when no one wants them.

6.4 Classical *utilitarianism* appears to be a much better candidate for explaining IO intuitions regarding the killing of young children. For it entails that such killing is wrong, at least in many instances, because it leads to a diminution of future pleasure. But the trouble here is that it also runs counter to IO intuition 2 – that artificial contraception is not normally wrong – in all of those cases in which not using it will result in an increase in future human pleasure by leading to the conception of future human receptacles of pleasure who otherwise would not have been conceived. Moreover, classical utilitarianism has the distressing consequence that we should see to it that, say, many more cows are brought into the world, so that they can experience the pleasure of grazing. (The latter consequence will no doubt deter conservative Roman Catholics from rejoicing over the former one.)

Desire-utilitarianism, on the other hand, is not thus future-oriented, since beings who are not yet conceived do not exist and, hence, do not have desires. It does, of course, entail that normally people who *desire* to have children for whom they can provide should be permitted to do so. But that is a far less extravagant consequence than the classical-utilitarian thesis that we should fill the earth with receptacles of pleasure. Moreover, desire-utilitarianism entails that it is *prima facie* morally wrong to kill beings who desire to live and, hence, that it is wrong to kill young children who have that desire, even when no adults desire to raise them. Desire utilitarianism is, then, the best account of intuitions 1 and 2.

6.5 However, my defence of desire-utilitarianism is not complete. For there are insuperable objections to *standard* versions of that theory, i.e. to the claim that only the number, duration and degree of intensity of our desires, the likelihood of their being satisfied by some course of action, and the effect of the present satisfaction of desires on future desire-satisfaction should be considered when we are making up our mind about what is morally correct. One such criticism of standard utilitarianism is that it entails an intolerable degree of moral laxity, since it entails, say, that telling deliberate falsehoods is morally justified, even in cases in which there is only a slight net gain in desire-satisfaction, and that, for example, the same is true of promise-breaking.

The so-called 'rule-utilitarian' attempts to meet this criticism by claiming that *more* desire-frustration will occur if we make a policy of lying and promise-breaking in such cases, rather than adhering to a rule which prohibits lying and promise-breaking. But this is not a satisfactory response. A common, and surely sound, rebuttal of it is that no one but a fanatic would wish there to be an *absolute* ban on the contemplated actions. For example, only a fanatic would think that breaking a promise to meet a friend for lunch would be morally bad, even if the only alternative was the death by torture of another friend. So the rule-utilitarian needs to formulate his rules of behaviour in such a way as to accommodate legitimate exceptions to that behaviour; and then, *qua* standard utilitarian, he finds himself unable to provide a satisfactory answer to the question of why he should not qualify his rules so thoroughly that there is no distinction between them and the simple rule which the so-called 'act-utilitarian' applies to telling falsehoods and promise-breaking, i.e. 'Maximize desire-satisfaction and minimize desire-frustration.'

IO intuitions about the killing of young children are also relevant here. Since it would obviously be wrong to kill a single, unwanted child simply because his desire to continue living is outnumbered by more intense or fecund desires that he be killed, standard utilitarianism also entails an intolerable degree of laxity with respect to doing away with young children.[1] Or, rather, as will become clear in 6.6, it entails an intolerable degree of moral laxity with respect to the young child's desire for continued life when this is *not* coincident with a desire to be saved from death by the heroic measures of strangers.

The best alternative to standard desire-utilitarianism is the view that, *while net desire-satisfaction is a touchstone of the moral goodness and badness of our actions, some net desire-satisfactions should be favoured over other net desire-satisfactions when there is a conflict of desires; and desire-preference in those cases should be determined by IO intuitions.* Thus, I should give your desire that I keep my promise preference over other, conflicting desires when the satisfaction of the latter desires will constitute only a slight gain in net desire-satisfaction; so, too, for your desire not to be given deliberately false information by me; and, in the case of the killing of a young child, I ought to give a higher priority to the present – or future – desire of the child for continued life than to the conflicting, more intense desires of others that I kill him.

Let me emphasize that by 'ought', in these contexts, I do not mean 'ought' from a utilitarian point of view. For that would be circular. What I mean, rather, is that IOs would disapprove of my not giving priority to the envisaged desire for continued life, and so forth. And, of course, we can generalize: all correct desire-ranking is based on IO intuitions.

6.6 Non-standard desire-utilitarianism (which I shall henceforth call simply 'non-standard utilitarianism') can enable the utilitarian to meet another familiar objection: namely, that utilitarianism, though it is too lax with respect to telling falsehoods and promise-breaking, is too *stringent* with respect to satisfying the desires of strangers, when the only alternative is curtailing the satisfaction of one's own desires or the desires of such non-strangers as one's children. For surely IOs normally favour one's satisfying the desires of one's children *more* than they favour one's satisfying the conflicting desires of strangers, and surely they normally do not *dis*favour one's satisfying one's own desires rather than the conflicting desires of strangers (though it is, perhaps, implausible that they normally *positively* favour one's satisfying one's desires *more* than they favour one's satisfying the desires of strangers).

I use 'normally' advisedly. If I encounter a stranger whose desire for life conflicts only with my desire to get to class on time or with my daughter's desire that I help her prepare dinner, then I clearly ought to prefer satisfying the stranger's desire to satisfying the former ones, i.e. IOs would favour my satisfying the stranger's desire, even though my doing so conflicts with my satisfying the other desires instanced. However, this does not entail that it is after all true that non-standard utilitarianism is, like standard utilitarianism, too strenuous. For, if I encountered *a large number* of strangers who were in danger of imminent death, then my life-saving efforts on behalf of *each* of them would *not* just frustrate relatively *trivial* desires of mine and of people such as my daughter, and no IO would intuit that I should none the less engage in those life-saving efforts. And the same is, of course, true of the many millions of starving strangers which the world contains and whom I do not personally encounter.

In conjunction with the IO-intuitive claim that it is normally wrong to take steps to harm people or to kill them, the foregoing entails that not helping or saving people (omitting to help or save them) is frequently better than harming or killing them (*committing* the act of harming or killing them). Standard utilitarians sometimes maintain that it is a theoretical virtue of their view that it cannot accommodate this distinction. But surely it is *strongly intuitive* that I am not morally obliged to render myself and my family destitute in a heroic attempt to save as many lives in Mozambique, Ethiopia, the Sudan and Bangladesh as I possibly can. And, *pace* some standard utilitarians, the contradictory thesis does not follow from the plausible assertion that I am morally obliged to save this or that stranger – for example, a child who is drowning in a nearby shallow pond – when only *trivial* desires of mine or those close to me need to be sacrificed. Thousands of drowning children in thousands of nearby shallow ponds are quite another matter, however. Peter Singer maintains in this connection that the only difference between the desperately needy strangers whom I personally encounter in my everyday life and those desperately needy strangers whom I do not personally encounter is *distance*; and he correctly maintains that distance *per se* does not constitute a morally relevant difference.[2] But distance *generates* a morally relevant difference, since the *number* of needy strangers multiplies with distance, and my obligations to come to their aid diminish as their number increases.

I have said in effect that an unwanted young child's desire for continued life should normally not be frustrated. But it is now clear that this claim needs qualification. The (relatively sophisticated) desire to be saved by the heroic measures of strangers is *not* such that we are obliged to honour it, though, of course, for its *parents* to make a strenuous, long-term effort to keep it alive may well be obligatory, even when they are disinclined to make that effort.

6.7 It may be thought that the prior section commits one who accepts it to political conservatism with respect to political redistribution of wealth. But in fact this is not so. For surely all or most IOs intuit that the desire of people to escape extreme poverty takes precedence over the desires of other people to live in extreme luxury. Thus, at least most IOs intuit that, even though democracies are apt to be more desire-satisfying than tyrannies, even democratic states in which a sizable number of people are very rich, while others are very poor, are, to that extent, morally defective (when it is *not* the case, as it sometimes is, that the misery of a very poor person is due to a culpable lack of prudence). Also, it is, I think, clear to at least many IOs that a way of maintaining a reasonably healthy economy, without massively promoting hedonistic consumerism via advertising, should be found, since the latter undoubtedly gives rise to frustrated desires on the part of people who would not have those desires in a less materialistic society.

Finally, it is surely clear to all qualified moral judges that the desires of those who suffer because of past or present desire-frustrating institutions should take precedence over the desires of people who have knowingly benefited from one or more of those institutions.

6.8   Another objection to non-standard utilitarianism is as follows:

Suppose (1) that someone, S_1, to whom another person, S_2, has no obligation-creating special relationship, ranks a desire, D_1, of his daughter above a *conflicting* desire, D_2, of S_2's son, and (2) that S_2, who has no special obligation-creating relationship to S_1, ranks D_2 above D_1. Then non-standard utilitarianism entails that *both* S_1, and S_2 are correct, which entails in turn that two desires, the conjunction of which cannot be satisfied, are such that the SPIO favours the satisfaction of D_1 and, hence, the frustration of D_2, and *also* favours the satisfaction of D_2

and, hence, the frustration of D_1. But surely the SPIO would neither (arbitrarily) favour the satisfaction of D_1 more than the satisfaction of D_2 nor (arbitrarily) favour the satisfaction of D_2 more than the satisfaction of D_1. Surely he would, in the envisaged circumstance, be *indifferent* about *which* desire is satisfied. But, then, neither S_1 nor S_2, who are *not* thus indifferent, can be IOs, even though their desire-ranking is, given non-standard utilitarianism, correct. And we are owed an explanation of that.

The reply is that S_1 and S_2 can be IOs without having an attitude toward satisfying D_1 and D_2 which is the same as the attitude of the SPIO. The reason for this is that the SPIO does not resemble human beings in having special obligations to biological offspring, human friends, students, colleagues, and the like. It does not follow, however, that human IOs can have attitudes which are *opposed* to some of the attitudes of the SPIO. For, though he cannot favour the satisfaction of both D_1, and D_2, he *can* favour S_1's *pro attitude* toward satisfying D_1, and $S2$'s *pro attitude* toward satisfying D_2.

What I have just said should be qualified as follows. If D_1 and D_2 are *trivial* desires, then indifference on the part of S_1 and S_2 is perfectly justified. But suppose that 'S_1's daughter needs an expensive life-saving operation, and so, too, does S_2's son. Surely in *that* case S_1 ought not to pay for S_2's son's operation, and *vice versa* (unless, of course, they swap expenses).

6.9 The standard utilitarian may wish to argue that the non-standard version can in fact be reduced to standard utilitarianism on the ground that (1) altruism is in short supply and, hence, (2) the number, duration, intensity, fecundity and likelihood of satisfaction of desires are in fact best served by the prioritizing of desires which I have been discussing.

But this argument can be rebutted as follows.

(a) As I pointed out in 6.5, the standard utilitarian criteria of desire-satisfaction entail unacceptable laxity with respect to killing unwanted young children and the present objection does not mitigate that fact.

(b) It is not relevant to the question of why lying and promise-breaking are wrong in cases in which they bring about a slight net gain in desire-satisfaction.

(c) The argument breaks down the IO-intuitive distinction between obligation and supererogation, for it entails that, when altruism is *not* in short supply, as in the case of Mother Teresa, one is simply doing what one morally ought to do by bringing about a net increase in desire-satisfaction. Here it may be said that supererogation can be plausibly interpreted as doing what is over and above what *ordinary* people do by way of desire-satisfaction. But suppose that a person with a large family suddenly becomes as altruistic with respect to strangers as is Mother Teresa. Surely it is false that he would then have no more stringent obligations to satisfy the relatively trivial desires of his children than to satisfy the less trivial desires of strangers (assuming that his children are not *themselves* Mother Teresas whose relatively trivial desires do not conflict with the less trivial desires of strangers).

(d) If the present standard utilitarian argument is correct, then it is a mere *coincidence* that present moral rules yield as great a net satisfaction of desires as human nature allows. For surely no experts have made, and acted on, a careful calculation that this is so. The upshot is that standard utilitarianism is committed to the strange conclusion that we should give our children a more strenuous moral upbringing in order to see whether we can achieve a gain in net desire-satisfaction and, if that does not work, then a *less* strenuous moral education in order to see whether we can *increase* respect for those moral principles which we finally decide to teach permanently. (The idea in the latter case is to avoid teaching a set of moral principles which, human nature being what it is, will tend to discourage respect for morality.)

6.10 Here someone may ask how IOs could possibly *know* that the kind of desire-ranking which I have been discussing is *correct*. One answer is that the standard utilitarian is himself subject to a similar question, i.e. 'How does he know that *his* criteria of desire-ranking are acceptable?' But we can answer the former question in a more direct manner: it is simply *self-evident* that our IO intuitions regarding desire-ranking should be trusted.

It may be objected at this point that, since it is a contingent fact that IOs have the intuitions which in fact they have, it *cannot* be a necessary truth that they rank conflicting desires as they do. But this is to overlook the fact that the ultimate criteria of moral correctness are the intuitions of God and that, as I argued in 4.4, it is a necessary truth that *some* of his intuitions are as they are. For it is a short step from there to the conclusion that it is a necessary truth that his intuitions regarding desire-ranking are as they are.

6.11 Two points remain to be made.

1 A well-known argument against standard utilitarianism is that, for all we know, actions which we are morally obliged to perform will lead to more desire-frustration than desire-satisfaction in the non-

immediate future. But, since, as I argued in 4.3, God wants us to make (many) *true* moral judgements, he does not permit it to be often the case that we believe falsely that actions which we take to be on balance desire-satisfying give rise in the long run to a net increase in desire-frustration.

2   It may be said here that, since God is both omnipotent and perfectly good, he would not permit there to be conflicting desires, since these frequently give rise to desire-frustration. And the objection can be enlarged on as follows: 'If God exists, then at least *his* moral goodness does not have his being a maximal desire-satisfier as a necessary condition, since even a cursory glance at our world shows that it is full of desires which are not fulfilled, even though an omnipotent being *could* fulfil them.'

But my discussion of the problem of suffering in 3.1 and 5.11 can be amplified in such a way as to provide an answer to this objection. Either *E* of 3.1 should be taken to be such an immense satisfaction of desires (including, perhaps, the desires of non-human beings) that it overrides desire-frustration or, given that desire-frustration results from the misuse of their free will by created moral agents, it remains true, even in view of this misuse, that their having free will is on balance more desire-satisfying than would be their not having it, since most free moral agents obviously prefer possessing that status to not possessing it.

6.12   We have just seen that desire-utilitarianism *per se* need not succumb to some well-known objections. And in Chapter 9 I shall mount a more positive defence of it by showing that it enables us to account for IO intuitions regarding the so-called 'doctrine of double-effect'. However, it is necessary to discuss first the morality of infanticide.

7 Infanticide, I

7.1 It may be thought that even non-standard desire-utilitarianism should be rejected on the ground that it cannot account for the obvious *prima facie* wrongness of killing unwanted neonates, who do not yet have a concept of themselves as continuing entities and, hence, cannot yet desire continued life. Now, I think that in fact there is a strong *prima facie* case against killing unwanted neonates, but in recent years a number of philosophers, most notably, Michael Tooley,[1] have defended infanticide; and we need at this point to examine the best of those defences. If they are in fact sound, then, of course, desire-utilitarianism need *not* account for the putative wrongness of infanticide.

In the course of his arguments, Tooley considers a number of examples and counter-examples, some of which make reference to Frankensteinian monsters and to kittens with a potentiality for developing into beings with a complex, normal human consciousness. These tend, I think, to muddy our intuitions, and I have replaced them with less bizarre examples of a biologically normal adult human being who has been in a coma all her life and of severely retarded human infants. These new examples have the virtue of being better clarifiers of our intuitions, while not distorting the main thrust of Tooley's argument.

7.2 Tooley correctly maintains that we can wrongfully harm a being only if we deprive him of something which he desired in the past or desires now or will desire in the future. (I have in effect defended this view in Chapter 6). Let us look first at what Tooley says about future desires. Suppose that some music-lovers painlessly castrate a boy soprano who has not in the past, and does not now, desire not to be castrated, but who, in the normal course of events, *will* come to desire sexual maturity. Because he will exist at a future time when that desire will be frustrated, the music-lovers seriously wrong him in present time. Moreover, consider the case of a female child whom her parents condition in such a way, while she is growing up, that she does not come to desire, as a biological adult, to be more than a passive helpmate. Then, even though her parents' treatment of her does not result in a future frustrated desire, as in the case of the boy soprano, they have none the less wronged her because she wil exist at a future time when she *would* have desired to be a fully fledged adult person, had they not brought her up to be simply a homemaker.

But now suppose that the boy soprano does not satisfy what I shall call 'Tooley's future-existence clause': suppose instead that he is dying of an incurable disease which will take his life before he would have come to desire sexual maturity. Then the music-lovers do not wrong him by castrating him in present time. And so, too, for the female child. If she will die as a child, then it is false that she will become an adult and *a fortiori* false that she would have had such and such adult desires. So her parents do not wrong her by treating her in the envisaged manner. But now infants, who are too young to have a concept of themselves as entities that continue over time, *do* not desire continued existence and, if we kill them, *will* not have such a desire. Hence, they do not satisfy Tooley's future-desire clause and so, according to Tooley, infanticide is morally justified.

But, of course, things are not so simple. And Tooley recognizes this, though not to an adequate extent. He asks us at this point to consider a case of a suicidally depressed patient who requests that his psychiatrist kill him, even though his psychiatrist is convinced, for good reason, that this patient will eventually recover and once again desire continued life. Plainly, it would be seriously wrong for the psychiatrist to acquiesce here, though it is also clear that, if he did, then the contemplated patient would, like a dead infant, not satisfy the future-desire clause. But Tooley thinks that he can successfully deal with this example by maintaining that the suicidally depressed patient differs in a morally relevant way from the neonate in that he *has* desired continued life in the past, i.e. Tooley adds to his (present) and future desire clause what I shall call 'a past-desire clause'. And he claims that it is crucial that, while the suicidally depressed patient satisfies it, the infant does not.

7.3 Is Tooley justified in adding the past-desire clause? Perhaps he thinks so because he believes (1) that the case of the dying boy soprano justifies the future-desire clause and (2) that it would, none the less, be wrong to castrate him in present time if, even though he *will* not desire sexual maturity in the future if we castrate him now, he has in the past desired sexual maturity (or, at any rate, has desired not to be castrated). Now, I submit that it is far from clear that *that* particular past-desire clause is *relevant* here, i.e. that we *would* be obliged to honour *that* past desire in the case now before us. But it is open to Tooley to reply here that I am right about the *special status* of the desire not to be killed (see 6.5) and that, hence, it is plausible that a prior desire *not to be killed* should be honoured in the present, regardless of what may be thought of a present desire not to be castrated.

But, even thus modified, Tooley's position is hard to accept. Suppose that Jones has had a strong desire all his life not to be killed, but of late has become a human vegetable, without the slightest chance of recovering from that condition. Would it really be wrong (painlessly) to kill him because of his vegetable state, even though he has had a prior desire for life?

But, for those who are morally opposed even to killing human vegetables, there is another objection. Even if having had a prior desire not to be killed is a morally sufficient condition for not killing an individual (for example, the suicidally depressed patient) in present time, it is surely not a *necessary* condition. Consider the case of a woman who has been in a deep coma all her life, and hence has never desired not to be killed, but about whom we know that she will, if we do not kill her, become conscious, and desire not to be killed, in a few minutes. Surely the mere fact that she has never desired not to be killed in the past would not justify our killing her just before she awakens from her coma.

But now what about Tooley's argument for his crucial *future*-desire clause? Isn't he clearly right that, if the boy soprano will die before he can desire sexual maturity, then we are justified in painlessly castrating him in present time? The answer is that it is plainly true that we are so justified, if his death will result from a fatal disease over which we have no control. But suppose that he will not be alive in the future because *we deliberately* bring about his death now. Then Tooley would simply be begging the question on behalf of infanticide were he to maintain that, even under those circumstances, castrating the boy soprano and then killing him would not, in its entirety, be wrong.

7.4 There is still another of Tooley's arguments[2] which we need to examine.

> Suppose that we are scientists who discover a drug which, when given to a severely retarded human infant, will bring it about that it will, in the near future, develop into a being who desires continued life. And suppose that we inject one of two severely retarded human infants with this drug, but fail to give it to the second one. Surely we are morally justified in omitting to give the second infant the drug and, hence, *would* have been justified in failing

to give the drug to the first infant. But if we would have been so justified, then we would *also* be justified in giving a *neutralizing*-agent to the first unwanted infant after we injected it with the drug. And there is no morally relevant difference between thus neutralizing the first infant and painlessly killing it. Hence, we are morally justified in painlessly killing unwanted infants who do not *require* a drug in order to develop a desire for continuing life.

What shall we think of this argument? Some may wish to maintain here that there is normally a morally relevant difference between omission and commission and, hence, that it does not follow just from the fact that it is admissible to *omit* to give the second infant the drug that it is also admissible to give the first infant a neutralizer. And others may wish to claim that there is a morally relevant difference between neutralizing the first infant and killing it. But, though I think that there is sometimes a morally relevant difference between omission and commission (see 6.6), I doubt that it obtains here. And I shall not pursue the question of whether killing is worse than neutralizing in the contemplated case. Rather, I shall say a few words about whether in fact we would be within our moral rights in failing to give the drug to either infant (plainly, if it is all right to fail to inject the one, it is all right to fail to inject both), and then I shall proceed to come more directly to grips with Tooley's argument.

Would it be all right to fail to give the drug in the first place? Suppose, to begin with, that it is scarce. Then giving it to just this or that particular infant would not, I think, be morally required but, *pace* Tooley, it is *not* clear that we would be morally justified in not giving it to *any* severely retarded human infant at all. But set that consideration aside, and suppose that the drug is as plentiful as say, water. Then there will be no non-arbitrary and non-preposterous answer to the question 'How many severely retarded infants must we inject with the drug?' For example, 'Just eight' will be arbitrary, and 'All the severely retarded infants there are' will be preposterous: surely we would not have a moral obligation to render ourselves destitute by spending all of our waking hours injecting severely retarded infants. So, in case the drug is very *plentiful*, it would be morally admissible not to give it to anyone.

But nothing of interest follows from that. For things are quite different once we *have* administered the drug. Though it may have been morally admissible *not* to have given the drug to the first infant in the first place, it simply does not follow that, having once injected the first infant, it is morally all right to give it the neutralizer and/or to kill it. For it surely does not follow from the fact that it *would* have been all right for me *not* to marry a woman in the first place that, *once I have done so*, it is morally admissible for me to be a philanderer, nor does it follow from the fact that I would have justifiably failed to promise to meet you in my office at 5 p.m. that it is acceptable to *break* that promise *once I have made it*. And so Tooley needs to tell us (but does not) why things should be otherwise, once in fact we have given the drug to the contemplated infant.

It follows that Tooley's second defence of infanticide is as defective as his first one.

7.5 Judith Thompson, though she appears to hold a feminist view of abortion, in fact lays the basis for another defence of infanticide. Her well-known fable of the women who, because of her rare blood type, has been kidnapped and had her circulatory system attached to that of a famous violinist who will die unless he remains attached to her ('back to back in bed') for nine months[3] evidently is intended to support her claim that 'having a right to life does not guarantee having either a right to be given the use of, or a right to be allowed continued use of, another person's body – even if

one needs it for life itself'.[4] (Though it has appeared to
some that Thompson's analogy supports only abortion due
to rape, she maintains, surely correctly, that it would be
grossly discriminatory to claim that *only* such foetuses
can be aborted, and that all others have a right to life,[5]
rather as though someone maintained that it is all right to
kill two-year-old children who are the products of rape.)
But Thompson adds that 'nobody is morally required to
make large sacrifices, of health, of all other interests and
concerns, of all other duties and commitments ... for ...
nine months, in order to keep another person alive'.[6] And
that second claim takes us beyond a purely feminist
approach to abortion.

Suppose that a woman finds herself in the following
predicament: she is compelled to make a long-distance call
to the violinist every day and to talk to him for several hours,
or the violinist will die. Here we do not have a case which
very much resembles the foetus's dependence on its
mother's body, but, if Thompson is right about one's not
being morally constrained to make large sacrifices to keep
another person alive, then the envisaged caller has no moral
obligation to talk to the violinist for several hours a day.
And the contemplated case *does* very much resemble the
case in which a mother who cannot give an infant up for
adoption (because, say, it is moderately retarded) is faced
with the option of either killing the infant or raising it at a
considerable sacrifice to herself.

Thompson later adds that

we do not have any [responsibility] for a person unless we
have assumed it, explicitly or implicitly. [But] if a set of
parents do not try to prevent pregnancy, do not obtain an
abortion, and then at the time of birth do not put it up for
adoption, but rather take it home with them, then they
have assumed responsibility for it, they have given it
rights, and they cannot *now* withdraw support from it at

the cost of its life because they now find it difficult to go on providing for it.[7]

And Thompson would wish to claim at this point that, if a mother has assumed responsibility for an infant by letting it be born, then it would normally be wrong for her to kill it.

But imagine that a pregnant woman and her husband have been in a coma since the inception of the woman's pregnancy and awaken just as the infant is born. Then they have not assumed responsibility (in Thompson's sense) for the neonate; and, hence, if Thompson is right, they would be justified in killing it, if they want neither to raise it nor to give it up for adoption.

Now, I think that Thompson's claim that we do not have responsibility for people for whom we have not assumed responsibility is mistaken. The case of the strange child who is drowning in a shallow pond shows otherwise. But do we have a responsibility to 'make large sacrifices' to raise a child whom we do not want to put up for adoption? The telephone variation on Thompson's violinist analogy appears to show otherwise.

But I think that in fact it does not. For hanging up the phone and walking away has the death of the violinist only as a side-effect, which may well be undesired, while killing an infant, by the means which are normally employed for the purpose of killing people – say, poisoning, stabbing, shooting or smothering – does not have the death of the infant as an undesired side-effect. And this makes a substantial morally relevant different between the two cases.

What I have just said is, of course, highly controversial, and therefore thoroughly in need of defence. But it will be convenient for me to put off that defence until the final section of Chapter 9, when I shall be much better prepared to discuss this matter.

8 Infanticide, II

8.1 In this chapter I shall argue two theses: first, that desire-utilitarianism can be enlarged in such a way as to accommodate the *prima facie* case against killing unwanted neonates, and, second, that in fact this enlargement is not merely *ad hoc*, since it enables us to overcome what would otherwise be a distressing impasse (which I shall consider in 8.5).

It will be convenient for me to give a step-by-step formulation of my enlargement.

1   As the neonate (and the developing foetus: call them *N*) continue to develop, they become more and more identical with a baby (call her *A*) who has a concept of herself and a desire for continued life, and with whose body *N*'s body is physically continuous. The degree of identity of *N* with *A* is a function of the degree to which *N* looks like *A*. Similarly, the block of marble, before it is worked on by the sculptor, is not identical with (or, anyway, has only a very low degree of identity with) the finished statue, though, as the changing marble comes more and more to resemble the finished statue, it becomes more and more identical with the latter.

2   It is wrong (painlessly) to kill *N just because* it is wrong to kill *A*. This is because it is wrong (painlessly) to kill living beings who do not desire continued life only if they *will*, if not killed, desire continued life in the future; and surely it is part of the best explanation of that fact that, *unless* it were wrong to kill beings who *do* desire continued life, it would *not* be wrong to kill beings who temporarily do not.

3   The degree of wrongness of killing *N* is a function of (a) the degree of wrongness of killing *A* and (b) *N*'s degree of

identity with A. The reason is that A exists at a given time, t, to a greater or lesser extent, depending on the degree at t of N's identity with A; and the wrongness at t of killing A is a function of the extent to which A exists at t.

Let me explain. N cannot be even partly identical with a non-existent thing. Hence, if N exists at t and at that time is partly identical with A, then A exists at t, even if, because N is destroyed, it does not exist *after* t. Now, since, at t, A exists just to the extent that N exists and N is not fully A, A only partially exists at t. And, the more identical with A N is at t the more completely does A exist at t and, hence, the greater the destruction of A which is involved in killing N. Moreover, the greater the destruction of A, the more wrong the killing of N.

Of course, if there were some independent ground for its being wrong to kill N, then killing N might be just as bad as, or worse than, killing A when she becomes fully A. (If, in destroying an uncompleted statue, we destroyed what was *per se* a beautiful work of art, then the wrongness of destroying the uncompleted statue might be just as bad as destroying the completed statue.) But, as I have argued in step 2, it is wrong to kill N only because it is wrong to kill A.

4   The claim that there are degrees of identity and existence is rendered plausible by the consideration that, for example, 'Jones, the sculptor, has partially completed a statue' does not, since it is an entirely unexceptional locution, predicate 'partially completed' of a non-existent object and so is plainly logically incompatible with 'It is false that there is a statue which Jones has partially completed.' The former sentence affirms that the completed statue exists but not fully, and, hence, that what Jones has brought about, which *does* fully exist, is identical with, but not *fully* identical with, the completed statue. The claim that, the greater the destruction of A, via the killing of N, the more morally wrong is the latter is, perhaps, *per se* less intuitive. But this much, at

least, can be said: the envisaged thesis is not *counter-intuitive*. And, that being so, it is, as will emerge in 8.5, rational to accept it.

5   It have said that 'Jones, the sculptor, has partially completed a statue' does not predicate 'partially completed' of a non-existent object. And someone may object that it does not follow that it predicates 'partially completed' of the *completed*, though only partially existent, statue, but rather than it predicates 'partially completed' of the partially completed statue. But this will not do. For, if 'Jones, the sculptor, has partially completed a statue' were best explicated by 'Jones has partially completed a partially completed statue', then the later sentence would expand into 'Jones has partially completed a statue which is partially partially completed', and so on *ad infinitum*. And, anyway, the claim that the contemplated explication captures the meaning of the original sentence (call it *S*), is obviously absurd.

A better objection is that *S* does not predicate 'partially completed' of anything, existent or non-existent, but rather simply affirms that Jones has produced a certain object – namely, a partially completed statue. My reply is that a partially completed statue is a statue which is partially completed, i.e. that 'Jones has produced a partially completed statue' itself predicates 'partially completed' of a statue. Reasonable people could, no doubt, disagree about this explication, were it not for the fact that, as we shall see in 8.5, there is a good reason for accepting it.

6   I have said in effect that, at *t*, *N* can be partly identical with *A*, even if, because *N* is destroyed, *A* does not exist *after t*. And it may be objected that I am therefore committed after all to the absurd conclusion that *N* can be partly identical with a non-existent thing – namely, fully existent *A*. My reply is that in fact fully existent *A* *does* exist in the envisaged case, but *only partially*. But, for the benefit of

doubters, I can dispense with that reply as follows. Consider the case in which A does fully exist after t. An *unsuccessful attempt* at t to kill N, which is partly identical with (fully existent) A, would normally be to some extent morally wrong, because it would be an attempt to kill A, which, since N is partly identical with A at t, partially exists at t. And it follows that a *successful* attempt to kill N, which *would* have been partly identical with A, had the attempt been unsuccessful, would also normally be to some extent morally wrong. For a mere lack of success cannot amount to a morally relevant difference.

7   I have said that, when N is physically continuous with A, it becomes more and more identical with A as it comes more and more to look like A. But suppose that we kill N. Then in fact it is *not* physically continuous with A. So, if it is a necessary condition of its being wrong to kill N that its body is physically continuous with A's body, then my partial-identity thesis does not, in fact, entail that infanticide is normally wrong. But it is a simple matter to accommodate this counter-example: it is a condition of its being to some extent wrong to *try* to kill N that *either* N's body *will* be physically continuous with A's body (since the attempt fails) *or it would have been* physically continuous with A's body *if* it had been allowed to develop. (If A were a person who could remember many of N's experiences, this condition might not be necessary, since it may be that P_1's remembering many of P_2's experiences, plus, perhaps, P_1's frequently behaving exactly like P_2, is a sufficient condition of P_1's being partially identical with P_2, even in the – logically possible – absence of physical continuity. Henceforth, the reader should mentally fill in the requisite negative qualification.)

8   Suppose that, though N's body is physically continuous with A's body, N does *not* resemble A because (what is logically possible), at the instant that N becomes fully

identical with A, A, though self-conscious, changes its appearance. Suppose, for example, that A becomes a self-conscious dolphin at that instant. In view of the fact that A, though a dolphin, desires continued life, killing N in the envisaged circumstances would be as bad as killing N in the case where no such transformation will take place. Here, I need to qualify still further: 'In the event that A, is, for example, a self-conscious dolphin and N is humanoid, the fact that N *would* have looked like A, if the sudden transformation had not occurred, entails that it is (to some extent) wrong to kill N.'

9   I have been taking it for granted throughout this section that, *pace* Hume, there *is* such a thing as identity over time. If Hume is right, then of course my account of *partial* identity is worthless. But there are two things to be said here. First, the concept of identity over time is deeply entrenched in common sense and, hence, there is a very strong *prima facie* case for it. Secondly, an argument in its favour is that it is far from clear why we should think it *prima facie* wrong to kill, for example, an unconscious adult if we reject the thesis that she, that very same woman, will desire continued life in the future if we do not kill her.

10   It may be said that the following is a counter-example to my claim that N's physical continuity with, as well as resemblance to, A provides a reason for thinking that it is *prima facie* wrong to kill N: 'It does not follow from the fact that it is wrong to operate on me when I am *not* anaesthetized that it is wrong to operate on me when I *am* anaesthetized, even though the anaesthetized Dore is physically continuous with, and resembles, the non-anaesthetized Dore.' But this case is very different from the case of N and A. In *that* case A desires continued life, or would have desired continued life it we had not killed N. In the anaesthetization case, the non-anaesthetized Dore has no

desire which is frustrated by one's anaesthetizing Dore at an earlier stage.

11 Still, my objector may press his case as follows: 'While *psychological* identity over time may well be relevant to the question of whether it is admissible to treat me now in such a way that some significant future desire of mine will be frustrated, it is obviously implausible that this is true of *physical* identity. And Dore must fall back on physical identity, since *ex hypothesi N* is not yet a person.'

One reply is simply that the counter-example of step 10 seems as good a candidate as can be imagined for demonstrating the envisaged implausibility claim, and that counter-example has been shown to be ineffective.

But there is another reply. The reason why it would be *prima facie* wrong to kill a deeply unconscious adult is that she will desire continued life upon becoming conscious again. But the criterion for '*she* will in the future desire continued life' is *ex hypothesi* not some *state of consciousness* which she is now in, and which she either has in common with her past self or *will* have in common with her *future* self. And the only plausible alternative criterion is physical continuity. Moreover, the case of *N* and *A* resembles the case of the deeply unconscious adult, thus characterized, in all relevant respects.

12 It may be thought that my (highly metaphysical) thesis that there are degrees of identity (for example, of *N* with *A*) can be replaced with the simpler (and less metaphysical) claim that, the more *N* resembles a self-conscious being (not necessarily *A*), the more difficult it becomes to justify killing *N*. But there appears to be no reason to accept this claim. For it is surely not in *general* true that, the more I look like a person of a certain kind, the more *prima facie* wrong it becomes to treat me in a manner in which it would be *prima*

facie wrong to treat people of that kind. Thus, my looking as though I am in pain has no relevance to the question of whether it would be wrong of you to chide me, if you have reason to believe that I am malingering; and, more to the point, even if I bore a striking resemblance to Mother Teresa, it would not be wrong of you to kill me in self-defence, nor would the stringency of your *prima facie* obligation not to kill me be increased, i.e. my resemblance to Mother Teresa has nothing to do with the matter.

8.2 Joel Feinberg has maintained in effect that, as a developing neonate takes on a more and more human shape, it becomes more and more difficult to justify killing it, not because it is at least partially identical with *A*, but because desire-satisfaction will be increased if people have respect for things with human shape and are, as a consequence, less apt to inflict harm on fully fledged human beings.[1] If Feinberg is right, then the above enlargement to desire-utilitarianism is unnecessary. However, Feinberg's view can be doubted. For killing a being who is in an irreversible coma is surely not wrong, even if it has a human shape. It may be said here, 'In fact we have a *prima facie* obligation *not* to kill human vegetables, but it is *overriden* by the consideration that they are using nourishment which others could benefit from, taking up precious space, and so on'. But the same will be true of the future stages of the developing neonate. And, anyway, would it really be wrong to kill a human vegetable just because it is *aesthetically displeasing*?

8.3 I mean to claim that it becomes more and more *prima facie* wrong to kill a developed foetus and a neonate as they come more and more to resemble a self-conscious baby.

And the conservative with respect to abortion may object as follows to that claim.

> Dore is right to maintain that it is wrong to kill *N* because killing *N* is killing *A* and killing *A* is wrong. But, if fitting the description 'killing *A*' is normally a sufficient condition for killing to be wrong, then killing the newly fertilized egg (call it *Z*), with whose body the bodies of *N* and *A* are physically continuous, would also be wrong, since *that* action also fits the envisaged description.

But in fact killing *Z* does *not* fit that description, for, if *Z* is killed, then *A* will never exist and *a fortiori* cannot be deprived of its existence. If *Z* were to some extent *identical* with *A*, then, since *Z* cannot be to some extent identical with *A* unless *A* to some extent exists, killing *Z* would be subjecting *A* to a degree of destruction. But, since *Z* does not at all *resemble A*, it is simply false that it is to *any* degree identical with *A*. And, even if they were not so, its degree of identity with *A* would be so negligible that killing it would not be seriously wrong.

The further objection that, regardless of whether *Z* is *identical* with *A*, its non-destruction is a necessary condition of *A*'s existence, and, when something is a necessary condition of the existence of another thing, then, if it would be wrong to destroy the latter, it is wrong to destroy the former, entails that artificial contraception is wrong, and hence it can be dismissed out of hand.

8.4   It is intuitive that *A*'s desire for continued life ought to take precedence over most other desires. But why should that be so? Why, for example, is it morally bad for a woman to satisfy her desire to go on an infant-free holiday by (painlessly) killing her new-born infant? Why should the fact that it will otherwise soon become a *life-desiring* person override her desire to go on holiday?

Let us consider first what are in effect standard desire-utilitarian attempts to answer these questions.

1   A person's continued life is a necessary condition of her satisfying many *other* desires.
2   The desire for continued life is, when one is conscious, more *intense* than most other desires.

Neither of these answers is acceptable. The trouble with answer 1 is that, if the *number* of satisfied desires is really relevant here, then – what is false – (a) we have a less stringent *prima facie* obligation to honour the desire for life of a person about whom we know that she has, say, two years to live than to honour the desire for life of a person about whom we know that she has, say, twenty years to live, and (b) we have a less stringent *prima facie* obligation to honour the desire for life of a single individual, when her desire conflicts with the more trivial desires of say twenty other people, than when her desire for life conflicts with the more trivial desires of, say, half that number of other people. And the trouble with answer 2 is that the strength of our *prima facie* obligation not to kill people who wish to live is not simply a function of *how much* they wish to live. Otherwise, we should have as stringent a *prima facie* obligation to honour a madman's very intense desire to see us, say, scratch our head as we do to honour a person's intense desire for continued life. Or, at any rate, the standard desire-utilitarian owes us an explanation of why that should not be true.

We have here, therefore, another reason for rejecting standard desire-utilitarianism in favour of its non-standard counterpart.

8.5   Though I think that the argument of 8.1 is plausible at face value, more can be done to render it plausible.

Consider the following version of the conservative's so-called 'slippery-slope' argument against abortion.

> Infanticide is clearly seriously wrong. But there is no morally relevant difference between the neonate and the foetus just before it emerges from the womb. And, so, too, for any stage of the developing foetus and the immediately preceding stage, until we slide all the way back to the newly fertilized egg (the zygote).

A standard liberal response to this argument is that its advocate cannot prevent it from taking us all the way back to the sperm–egg pair, which will unite to form the zygote (the gamete pair), and, hence, that it proves more than some conservatives desire: namely, the *extreme* conservative conclusion that artificial contraception is seriously wrong. John T. Noonan is a *moderate* conservative, i.e. a conservative with respect to abortion but not artificial contraception. Noonan in effect tries to meet the envisaged liberal response in two ways.[2]

1 The zygote has the genetic code of the future human being which it will become if it is not destroyed, while the gamete pair does not. And this stops the slide back to the latter: because of its DNA, there is a morally relevant difference between killing the zygote and preventing conception by the use of contraceptives.
2 There is a high probability that the zygote, if not destroyed, will become a fully fledged human person; but the likelihood of any given sperm and any given ovum becoming a zygote is enormously small.

However, these replies are not impressive. The trouble with reply 1 is that DNA molecules *per se* make no moral claim on us. Otherwise, it would be wrong to brush one's teeth or wash one's face, thereby killing some DNA-inhabited cells.

The DNA molecules which are contained in the zygote are, of course, different from those which are contained in one's teeth and face, since the former, but not the latter, will, in the normal course of events, become a human person. But this is true as well for the gamete pair. Reply 2 is even less impressive. Suppose that (as frequently happens) a woman has predictable fertile periods and her husband a normal, or above normal, sperm count. Then, though they cannot know specifically which of the multitude of sperms involved in an ejaculation will fertilize a given ovum, they can be quite certain that *some one* of them will. Uncertainty about a *given* sperm does not entail uncertainty about *all* of the sperms which are involved in the ejaculation. Hence, such uncertainty cannot be relevant to the question of whether artificial contraception is warranted. (Similarly, if I know that there are people in the hotel room next to mine and that at least one of them will be killed if I throw dynamite into the room, the fact that I don't know *which one* will be killed has no bearing on the question of whether I am justified in throwing dynamite into the room.)

Must we, then, accept the slippery-slope argument (call it 'SS1') and the extreme conservative position to which it commits those who accept it? Before doing so, we should consider a counterpart argument (which I shall call 'SS2').

The newly fertilized ovum plainly does not have a right to life. But, now, there is no morally relevant difference between the zygote at a given moment, *M*, and the developing organism a few moments later. And, so, too, for any stage of the developing organism and the immediately *succeeding* stage, until we slide all the way to, say, a three-month-old baby, who desires continued life. Hence killing the three-month-old baby (painlessly) is morally admissible.

One reply to this parody is that in fact the zygote *does* have a right to life. But, as I have pointed out, it is far from clear why one who makes this claim is not committed to the unpalatable thesis that even the gamete pair has a right to life. I submit, therefore, that the *best* explanation of what is wrong with SS2 is, in fact, as follows: though the differences between temporally very close stages of the developing organism are very small, the *sum* of those differences over a period of months is very great. A defender of SS2 would be like a person who argued that there is no difference between an oak tree and an acorn, on the ground that the differences between temporally very close stages of the developing tree are very small. She would be overlooking the fact that the *sum* of these small differences is *not* a small difference. But, now, since there is a *substantial* difference between the zygote and the gamete pair on the one hand, and the self-conscious baby on the other, the claim that, since it is morally admissible to kill the former, it is morally admissible to kill the latter, can be seen to be a *non sequitur*.

It is clear, however, that this refutation of SS2 gives the defender of SS1 no ground for rejoicing. For the very same refutation applies *mutatis mutandi* to SS1: the *sum* of the very small differences between the immediately preceding stages of the organism, when we are tracing the neonate in thought back to the zygote and the gamete pair, is *not* a very small difference; so the claim that, since it is wrong to kill the neonate, it is wrong to kill the zygote and the gamete pair, is clearly a *non sequitur*.

Still, there is another, more impressive version of the slippery-slope argument (call it 'SS3').

It will not do for the non-conservative simply to affirm that it is not, at all stages of the developing organism, wrong to kill it. She needs to tell us at *precisely what* stage it becomes no longer wrong to kill it and precisely *why* it is no longer wrong to kill it at that stage. If she cannot do so, then aborting at *any* stage, and, indeed, even regularly using artificial contraception, is morally risky. And repeatedly performing morally risky actions is doing something which is morally wrong. (This last consideration disposes of SS2-type parodies.) But the most plausible attempt to specify a stage at which preventing the existence of a future person is morally acceptable, namely, at the zygote stage, is, as Dore concedes, a failure. Hence, extreme conservatism can after all be vindicated.

Now it may well be said here that the following argument is at least as persuasive as SS3.

It is, at the very least, no *more* likely that, for example, a zygote has a right to life than that a pregnant woman, *W*, has a right to determine what happens to an organism which is parasitical upon her body. It follows that it is, at least, no *more* likely that we are violating a zygote's right to life by aborting it than we are violating *W*'s right to biological self-determination by preventing her (by force or persuasion) from having an abortion.

This argument is a kind of *tu quoque* with respect to SS3, since it appears to support the conclusion that *accepting* conservatism is *also* morally risky. But we are at a distressing impasse here and one which we should surely overcome if we can. And I submit that the moral gradualism of 8.1 is the best way of coping here. For there is evidently no precise cut-off point beyond which it becomes for the first time morally acceptable to abort a developing foetus or infant.

8.6 In his well-known paper 'I Do Not Exist' Peter Unger argues that there are no such things as tables and 'such alleged things as sticks and stones, mountains and lakes . . . ships and carriages . . . bodies of horses and of generals and so on and so forth'.[3] The following is a simple paraphrase of Unger's argument about tables.

> In the process of removing in thought atoms (or molecules or tiny splinters) from a putative table, we never reach a precise moment at which the putative table disappears. Hence, there never was a table in the first place.[4]

However, there is a plausible explanation of what is wrong with this radically sceptical argument. The argument of 8.1 gives us the basis for such an explanation. As more and more atoms are removed from the fully fledged table in Unger's thought-experiment, the table looks less and less like a table. And that entails that, as more and more atoms are removed, the table becomes less and less *identical* with the fully fledged table, until the envisaged entity bears no resemblance at all to that table, at which point, since it is not even partially identical with the original, fully fledged table, the latter ceases to exist.

9 The Doctrine of Double Effect

9.1 Consider the cases of the terror bomber and the tactical bomber.[1] The terror bomber kills innocent civilians because he believes that this is a causally necessary and sufficient condition of demoralizing the civilian population and, hence, shortening a just war. The tactical bomber, who drops bombs on a factory which produces materials which are important to the enemy's war effort, does so with the same end in view: namely, shortening a just war. He may, furthermore, firmly believe that his bombing of the factory will result in the deaths of some nearby, innocent civilians.

The terror bomber cannot regret the presence of civilians in the areas. He wants the war shortened, and firmly believes that there is no other way of shortening it than by dropping bombs on innocent people; and so he cannot say sincerely, 'I regret that there is anyone down there to be hit by bombs which I'm now dropping'; and, indeed, he cannot even say, 'I regret that those people are innocent', for he knows that, if they were not, then other non-combatants would not get the point. But the tactical bomber *can* sincerely regret the presence of the innocent civilians below. The reason for this difference is that, in the case of the tactical bomber, the death of innocent civilians is a *side-effect* of what he aims to do, whereas, in the case of the terror bomber, the death of innocent civilians is *not* a side-effect: it is his *aim*. He may, of course, regret the necessity of the just war in which he is participating; but this does not entail that he does not desire the deaths of the people below.

Many people think that what the terror bomber does is morally wrong, whereas what the tactical bomber does is not. (Even the US Defense Department denies that its nuclear weapons are intended to kill innocent civilians in the event of an outbreak of nuclear war.) Non-standard desire-utilitarianism can account for the contemplated difference: the terrorist bomber's desire to kill innocent people is outranked by the desires of innocent people not to be deliberately killed; but the tactical bomber does *not* desire to kill innocent people and *a fortiori their* desire not to be killed does *not* take precedence over his desire to kill them. (Indeed, it may be that the *standard* desire-utilitarian can adequately account for the contemplated difference, by pointing out that people who desire to kill in wartime situations are more likely to desire to kill in other contexts than are people who, like the tactical bomber, do not want innocent people to die.)

Someone may say here that in fact the terror bomber is not reprehensible, if his desire to kill the people below is based, like the tactical bomber's desire to bomb the factory, on a desire to shorten the war. But I submit that what the terror bomber does is akin to taking, and deliberately killing, hostages, and that the latter is normally morally wrong even when its perpetrator is motivated by a desire to avoid future killing.

But isn't it also true that the tactical bomber's desire to shorten the war does not justify him in performing an action which, though it is not an act of deliberate killing, has the deaths of innocent people as a foreseen consequence? The answer is that the desire of the innocent victims not to die stands to the tactical bomber's desire to shorten the war by bombing the factory as the desire of a total stranger to avoid death by being saved by me at a huge expense stands to my conflicting desire to see to it that my children have a college education. However, as the hostage analogy shows, the desire of an innocent stranger not to be deliberately killed by me normally takes precedence over any of my desires, no matter how intrinsically noble they may be.

9.2 Let us pursue this matter further. I submit that the following condition is satisfied in almost all cases in which, though a person foresees that innocent people will die as a result of what he is going to do, he none the less does not desire their deaths: the agent would do the same thing, and with the same motive, even if he knew that it would not cause any deaths. Thus, the tactical bomber would bomb the factory, and with the same motive, even if he knew that there were no innocent civilians nearby (and would feel much better about it), whereas it makes no sense to say that the terror bomber would drop bombs on innocent civilians, and with the same motive, even if he knew that there were no innocent civilians below. Call the 'would do it anyway, and with the same motive' condition *C*.

We need to qualify here. For consider the case, similar to one cited by Philippa Foot,[2] in which a fat man is blocking the entrance to a cave and, since the inhabitants will suffocate unless they dislodge the fat man by blowing him up, they in fact do so. Now, it is true that they would have blown the fat man up anyway, and with the same motive, even if they had known that this would neither have killed him nor even harmed him. But, if we agree that condition *C* is satisfied by *that* kind of highly bizarre counterfactual, then, of course, no one is *ever* justified in doing what he does by satisfying *C*. (Another case in which it is even clearer that one would be doing something wrong – since it is not a case of self-defence – is the case, cited by Gilbert Harman[3] and James Montmarquet,[4] in which a doctor cuts up one of his patients in order to obtain organs for five patients who will die otherwise. Presumably he would have cut the patient up anyway, and with the same motive, even if that would not have killed or even harmed him; but that consideration hardly justifies his action.) Plainly, then, the following constraint on *C* is needed: the satisfaction of *C* justifies someone in doing what he does only when the antecedents of the relevant counterfactuals are not such that it is causally impossible for them to be true. (For simplicity, I shall henceforth not explicitly refer to this qualification.)

If, as I have been maintaining, the satisfaction of C, in the case of the tactical bomber, and the non-satisfaction of C, in the case of the terror bomber, is the morally relevant difference between them, then it is clear that, though the terror bomber does what is morally inadmissible because he desires the deaths of innocent people, the tactical bomber does not desire the deaths of innocent people and, for that reason, does *not* do what is morally inadmissible. For it is obvious that a person who deeply regrets that his action has certain side-effects, and would perform that action anyway, and with the same motive, even if he could avoid those side-effects, does not desire those side-effects.

9.3 I have said that condition C is satisfied in all cases in which, though one foresees people's deaths as the result of what one does, one does not desire those deaths. And I have said in effect that, when one regrets those deaths, one does not desire them and, hence, cannot justifiably be blamed for them. These claims are demonstrably true.

Philippa Foot[5] and James Montmarquet[6] consider roughly the following case (first discussed by Foot): a runaway train will kill five people on the track ahead of it unless it is steered onto a side track, in which case it will kill one person. Foot, in whose example the option of the engineer's doing nothing at all is omitted, maintains (what is IO-intuitive) that he should steer into the one person, rather than into the five, because this involves a conflict between two negative duties (duties not to harm people), and there-fore should be decided on the basis of numbers. However, in cases of conflict between negative and positive duties (i.e. duties to benefit people), it is, according to Foot, wrong to violate the negative duties rather than the positive ones. Montmarquet builds into Foot's case the proviso that the engineer can do nothing at all if he so chooses, but that, if he fails to steer the train, it will certainly kill the five. And he adds that *this* kind of case raises

> an acute dilemma for Foot. Here the choice is not between steering into five and steering into one, but between steering into one and *letting* the train go into the five. And so the question arises, for Foot: Is the duty a matter of a positive duty to save their lives, then, contrary to Foot's own intuitions, it would be overridden by our negative duty not to kill the one. If, though, it is a negative duty, then we can have negative duties to those who would be harmed by our *in*action – in which case we need an explanation of why [a doctor does not] have a negative duty to [five patients whose lives depend on his cutting up another patient in order to obtain his organs].[7]

Montmarquet's own explanation of the contemplated IO intuition is that, while the patient whom the doctor contemplates cutting up for his organs is not already threatened with death, the man on the side track does have that status, and, hence, though killing the former would be wrong, killing the latter is morally acceptable.[8] Montmarquet cites another case which exhibits that feature: a madman in a crowd is shooting at the people around him, and you have no way to stop him except by throwing a grenade at him, in which case you will probably kill some other persons in the crowd (though not all of them). Here you are justified in throwing the grenade because the other people whom you will probably kill are already threatened with death.[9] (It might be argued that in fact the person on the side track is *not* already threatened, since, unless the engineer steers into him, the train will go straight ahead, and he will not die. But perhaps Montmarquet would say that the very presence on the train of an engineer with refined moral sensibilities *puts* the former person at risk.)

In any event, still another thought-experiment will show that the best account of the cases discussed so far is in terms of the fact that condition C is satisfied in both of them. First, the engineer would steer the train onto the side track, and with the same motive, even if no one were there. Secondly, the grenade-thrower would throw the grenade even if the madman were not in the midst of a crowd, but shooting at people from a distance. And, thirdly, imagine that there are five people on a life raft, all of whom will die of starvation within three days unless they bring aboard a large fish which they have caught. And imagine further that they know that they will be rescued in three days if they can stay alive. And, finally, imagine that they know that one of the five (call him 'Robinson') has a rare allergy, which will kill him if he finds himself in the presence of the fish. Surely, though it would be morally admissible to bring aboard the fish, even against Robinson's will, because doing so satisfies C (it would be brought aboard anyway, and with the same motive, even in the absence of Robinson, or even if he did not suffer from the allergy), it would be morally wrong to stab Robinson to death against his will a few moments before the fish arrived on board, even if one did so in order to prevent the fatal allergic reaction, since one's doing so would *not* have satisfied C. Montmarquet's explanation does not apply here: for the fact that everyone on the boat, including Robinson, is threatened with starvation is simply not relevant to the question of whether it is right or wrong to stab him to death.

Montmarquet also discusses a case,[10] first contemplated by Foot,[11] in which three patients, who cannot be moved, need an emergency operation to live; but, because of a malfunction in the operating-equipment, performing the operation will leak deadly gas into the next room, killing its lone inhabitant, who also cannot be moved – a person who is recovering well and will soon be released from hospital. Both Foot and Montmarquet maintain that it is intuitive that it would be wrong to perform the operation, but Foot explains this in terms of a negative duty not to kill the person in the next room; and Montmarquet, since he has expressed doubts about whether Foot's cases are all best explained in terms of negative duties, explains the case by pointing out that the person in the next room, unlike the persons in the crowd, who are threatened by a madman in their midst, is not already threatened. (Actually, there is a question as to why Montmarquet should not have to concede that, if the doctor in the case *will* in fact perform the operation, then the person in the next room *is* threatened by the former's presence. But let us set that aside.) If Montmarquet is right here, then, since performing the contemplated operation would satisfy condition *C* (the doctor would perform it, and with the same motive, even if the gas were not going to leak or if there were no one next door), the satisfaction of that condition cannot provide us with a explanation of all of the cases before us and, hence, we should suspect that it is not the correct explanation of any of them. But in fact I think that Foot and Montmarquet are both mistaken about the present case. First of all, Foot is mistaken if she thinks that the duty not to kill people, in the sense of doing something which has their death as a desired end, is operative here. For, once again, the operation satisfies condition *C*; and, when *C* is satisfied and the agent regrets the death involved, then the desire to bring about death is absent. And it is far from clear that an agent's action can be accurately described as an act of killing when death is an undesired side-effect. Moreover, I think that the intuitions of both Foot and Montmarquet about the case under discussion may well be based on the fact that the envisaged setting is a hospital, in which, though it is common for a doctor to *omit* to save people (for example, severely deformed infants and aged human vegetables), it is at least very rare for a doctor to *commit* actions which have as a foreseen consequence the deaths of patients. And I submit that, if we think of a case which is very similar, except that the setting is a two-room house on a desert island, our intuitions will tell us that performing the operation in *that* setting is not in fact morally wrong (so long as it is certain that two or more of the patients will recover). But, of course, the respective settings are not *per se* morally relevant. Therefore the hospital setting is intuition-muddying, i.e. it is not as IOs that we intuit that operating in *that* setting would be wrong. (Actually, Foot, Montmarquet and I have oversimplified the description of the case a bit. We need to know whether the three people who require the operation will, if they live, have at least the same potential for desire-satisfaction as the person in the next room. But that can be easily remedied: let us suppose that they will.)

9.4   Is what the terror bomber does wrong under *all* circumstances? Suppose that he acts as he does because of a justified belief that, unless he deliberately kills innocent people, many *more* innocent people will be deliberately killed in a prolonged and vicious way. Some IOs may think that even the terror bomber acts with moral justification in that case. And, of course, other IOs will deny this. (See Section 9.1.) I shall not try to adjudicate between these two positions here. Suffice it to say that, as I argued in 4.4, IO conflicts of this sort are very rare.

Many Catholic defenders of the doctrine of double effect disagree in effect with the claim that the tactical bomber, at least, is justified in killing *large numbers* of people, even though he regrets the deaths and also satisfies condition *C*. For example, the American Catholic bishops, in what is, for the most part, an admirably well-reasoned moral policy statement,[12] maintain that the massive destruction of civilians which would occur were the United States to use nuclear weapons to knock out an enemy's further war-making capacity would be morally unjustified, even if this came after a first strike on the United States. But I think that they are thereby unwittingly committed to the conclusion, surely distressing to any theist, that there is no adequate rebuttal of the atheistic argument from suffering. For I submit that the rebuttals of Chapters 2 and 5 are the only plausible rebuttals which are available. And, though neither of them contemplates God's bringing about a world in which there is widespread suffering without satisfying condition C (God would no doubt have brought about end E, and with a similar motive, even if suffering had *not* been a logically necessary condition of his doing so;[13] and, similarly, he would have created free moral agents even if no set of person-properties would have sinned when instantiated), they do essentially involve the claim that massive suffering is a side-effect of some of God's actions.

For my part, I am inclined to accept one of the rebuttals of the argument from suffering rather than agree that actions which have the foreseen consequence that deaths will result as a side-effect are always unjustified when a massive number of deaths and a huge amount of suffering are involved.

9.5 Non-standard utilitarianism, like standard utilitarianism, entails that capital punishment is wrong when the only motive is retribution. And I am committed by what I have said in 9.4 to the conclusion that, if capital punishment massively deterred murder, then it might appear to some IOs to be justified, despite the desire of the person who is executed not to be killed. But, whether or not capital punishment can be shown to deter murder to *some* extent, it is surely not a *massive* deterrent, and, hence, I am far from being committed to the conclusion that it is morally acceptable. And, it should be added, I am, unlike the standard utilitarian, not forced to accept the unpalatable thesis that it is morally admissible knowingly to convict an innocent man and then execute him, in order to prevent, say, a riot, so long as it is known that this will not become public knowledge. For it is open to me, as it is not open to the standard utilitarian, to maintain (what I am sure is true) that the desire of the innocent man not to be convicted and executed should take precedence over whatever desires would be frustrated were the riot to take place.

9.6 It is now time to return to Thompson. Suppose that in fact it is morally admissible for the woman in my modified version of Thompson's analogy to hang up the phone and walk away. Then this is because, in so doing, she would be satisfying condition C (she would have done so anyway, and with the same motive, even if the violinist had not been on the line or had not been going to die were she to hang up) and, hence, if she regretted hanging up, then she would not have desired his death. I contend, however, that, if she had killed the violinist by pressing a button which activated a bomb which blew him up before she could hang up, then moral matters would be different. For, under those circumstances, condition C would *not* have been satisfied and, hence, she would have *desired* the violinist's death. And, similarly, killing unwanted infants, by the means by which people are normally killed, does not satisfy condition C, so my modified version of Thompson's violinist case does not after all justify killing them. (Exactly similar considerations apply, of course, to Thompson's unmodified analogy. The fact that the woman in that analogy would have pulled the plug and walked away even if the violinist had not been going to die as a result entails that her doing so when the consequence *is* the death of the violinist, does not show that she desires his death – though, if she had to strangle the violinist or stab him in order to disconnect, then this would make matters morally different. Thompson maintains in effect that only a person who is confused by squeamishness would intuit that strangling or stabbing the violinist is morally worse than merely unplugging from him,[14] but the boat case which he contemplated toward the end of 9.3 shows that she is mistaken.

10 Moral and Non-Moral Value

10.1 A final objection to the Ideal Observer theory must now be considered.

> It is incredible that there is no overlap between moral and non-moral value. But the IO theorist cannot adequately account for this overlap. For it is preposterous to argue that, say, strawberries are good in the spring because the SPIO approves of them then. Surely the SPIO does not *eat* strawberries.

One reply is that the SPIO does favour strawberries in the spring (and good cups of coffee, good cameras, and so on), not because he consumes (or uses) them, but because he favours *human* desire-satisfaction and these things either satisfy human desire or are *potential* satisfiers of human desires. (I have in mind the strawberry which is never eaten.) Epistemic value – one's believing what one ought to believe – satisfies the desire for truth; and knowledge of the truth is a necessary condition of the satisfaction of many other human desires. Hence, the SPIO must also favour one's doing one's epistemic duty. (I do not want to assert here that all human beings have the very *strenuous* epistemic duties which scientists, epistemologists and the like impose on themselves. But I do maintain that there are some things which *every* rational being epistemically ought to believe.)

The *ranking* of non-moral values, as in '1982 was a better year for Cabernet Sauvignon than was 1984', has to do not just with human desire-satisfaction but with connoisseurship, i.e. with people who have experienced a wide range of wines (or whatever), and who prefer this one, or this kind, to that one, or that kind. And this is even more evident when we are dealing with the comparative value of works of art. However, it remains true that a *necessary* condition of non-moral value is potential for desire-satisfaction. And it is also the case that, with respect to the *ranking* of non-moral values, a kind of IO theory provides us with the best explanation. Hence, the IO theorist can account for the envisaged overlap: morality has to do with correctly ranked desire-satisfaction and so, too, has non-moral value.

But it is not enough just to point out what they have in common. We need also to know what distinguishes them. It may be thought that, when we evaluate not strawberries, wines and paintings, but desire-satisfying or desire-frustrating *human actions*, we are then *ipso facto* engaged in moral thinking. But reflection will show that this thesis is untenable. The doctor who in the course of pursuing his profession (for financial reward) prescribes a certain medicine for me is performing a desire-satisfying action, but not a morally good or bad one. And so, too, for the pharmacist who fills the prescription.

I submit that the correct account of moral value, as opposed to non-moral value, has roughly[1] to do with the *overriding importance* of the former, a feature of morality which every major moral philosopher from Plato on has stressed. We are in need, then, of an adequate account of overridingness.

10.2 In *Freedom and Reason* Richard M. Hare claims that 'There is a sense of the word "moral" (perhaps the most important one) in which it is characteristic of moral principles that they cannot be overridden . . . but only altered or qualified to admit of some exception.'[2] Hare does not believe (what is manifestly false) that, due to weakness of will, people cannot fail to conform their behaviour to principles which they take to be moral ones. So presumably he holds that overridingness consists in peoples not being able knowingly to break moral rules without feeling that they ought not to.[3] But, when we are dealing with a conflict between principles of *prima facie* obligation, we frequently violate one principle in order to conform to another, without believing that we have done something wrong. So Hare's characterization of moral principles is at best in need of the following qualification: 'Moral principles are overriding, except in cases when principles of *prima facie* obligation conflict and one is overridden by another.'

But, even thus qualified, Hare's analysis is mistaken. For there are surely extreme aesthetes who, though they think that a given principle is a moral principle, and one which they are not prepared to qualify, are disposed to violate it without any remorse in case of a conflict between that principle and, say, listening to a Mozart symphony.

In his more recent book *Moral Thinking*, Hare appears to concede that moral principles can be overridden without remorse.[4] He does not set the overridingness of morality aside, however, but gives the following, qualified account: *P* is a moral principle relative to a given individual, *S*, if and only either (a) *S* would let *P* take precedence over any *P*-violating course of action which he might consider, or (b), where *P* is not such a principle, 'critical thinking, however primitive' about *P* would lead *S* to justify *P* by appealing to at least one principle which *S* does treat as overriding, and hence, is for *S* a moral principle.[5] But surely we can *conceive*, at least, of an extreme aesthete who, though he takes 'Do not let harm befall a loved one in order to satisfy an intense aesthetic desire' (call this *Q*) to be a moral principle, feels no scruples about violating it. And Hare needs to tell us what principle, *P'*, it is which is such that (a) the envisaged aesthete takes it to be overriding and (b) critical thinking would lead him to justify *Q* by referring to *P'*.

10.3 Having in view Hare's failure to give an adequate account of the connection between morality and overridingness, I propose the following analysis.

> It is of overriding importance for a person, S, to perform a given action, A, if and only if (1) the SPIO would disapprove if S did not perform A, and (2) the SPIO favours that S should suffer harm for not performing A (harm greater than any harm that might result from his performing it).

On this analysis, non-moral value differs from moral value, since people who, say, fail to cultivate a taste for Bach and Mozart are normally not such that the SPIO disapproves of their failure to do so and favours their being harmed because of that failure.

Here I am attributing overridingness not to principles, but *to the importance of a person's performing certain actions*. Hence, even though an aesthete might violate Q without believing that he ought not to, it remains, on the present view, of overriding importance that he should not violate Q – not because he has scruples about the violation, but because he will be harmed as a result of it.

At this point a devout theist might object that condition (1) of my analysis is all that is required to account for the overridingness of morality, since doing what God disapproves of is unsurpassingly negatively momentous. But I submit that wrongdoers who mistakenly do not think so, and/or who take delight in doing what they believe that God disapproves of, are none the less subject to being harmed, in the sense that they are subject to something which they strongly desire to avoid. For surely the concept of morality is the concept of something which is such that it makes an important difference to a person's life whether he is relatively morally righteous or not, in a way which *he takes to be* an important difference. It follows that moral reprobates are harmed by undergoing what *they take to be harm*; and it follows in turn that their simply being indifferent to moral requirements (and, hence, in effect, to God's pro and con attitudes) is not the only harm which befalls them, even if that indifference can be properly characterized as *one* harm from which they suffer.

10.4 In the history of philosophy there have been a number of notable attempts to explain what kind of harm *does* befall evildoers, other than merely a loss of moral innocence. Plato's view, boiled down, is that, if S is a moral reprobate, then he is bound to suffer, because human psychology is such that moral evil inevitably gives rise to intolerable suffering, independently of whether one is punished by other people. But, stated thus baldly, Plato's theory appears to be patently false of highly powerful clever and prudent evildoers. (Powerful, clever and prudent evildoers will, of course, undergo suffering during their lifetime, but then so will all of us.)

Hobbesians, on the other hand, argue (more plausibly) that morality is overriding because the only alternative to it – a lack of restraint in pursuing what would be one's interests in a world without moral rules – would cause considerably more suffering than having and obeying moral rules does. But it is surely not *in all instances* true that wrongdoers suffer what is, by secular standards, significant harm as a result of their wrongdoing.

Let us pursue this latter point. It is plainly true that, if there were a being who was vastly shrewder and more powerful than any human being, and who tortured people just for fun, he could not, in view of his vastly superior power and shrewdness, fail to be doing what is morally bad. But, since he would be acting in a morally impermissible way, and since morality is overriding (in my sense), he would be harmed as a result, no matter how powerful and shrewd he might be. It is a necessary truth that moral badness is not a function of power and shrewdness: principles of moral decency are overriding in all possible worlds.

However, there could be no guarantee that the obligation not to torture people for fun would be overriding even for the contemplated evildoer (call him S) unless there were an inflicter-of-harm on the morally wicked who was even more powerful and knowledgeable than S. But this consideration points to an omnipotent and omniscient being. And simplicity dictates that we identify this being with God.

Here someone may ask what would be the case if S were *also* omnipotent and omniscient. The answer is that, as I argued in Chapter 4, the concept of God is such that it is a necessary truth that nothing can surpass or even rival him with respect to his perfections, unless he would be less perfect if some perfection of his could not be matched by other persons. But omnipotence and omniscience are not among the latter perfections. Hence, it is logically impossible for S to be omnipotent and omniscient.

It may be objected here that the concept of supererogation is a moral concept, though the nature of supererogatory action is such that one's refraining from performing a supererogatory action is not morally impermissible, and, hence, not subject to punishment (as is refraining from performing an action which is morally obligatory). But there is a plausible reply: supererogatory actions are moral actions not because God is disposed to *punish* people who fail to perform them, but because God is disposed to *reward* those people who do perform them.

10.5 The prior section gives rise to a reason for thinking that we survive bodily death: the *degree* of overridingness of our obligations is plainly a function of their degree of stringency. My obligation to try to cheer you up is plainly less stringent and overriding than my obligation not to kill you. Now, since relatively morally innocent people (starving children, for example) suffer at least as much as thoroughly evil people in this world, and since the overridingness of the obligations which are violated by the latter is greater than the overridingness of whatever obligations may be violated by the former, there must be an afterlife in which moral reprobates are punished *more* than the relatively innocent (given that the former have not been adequately punished in this world).

To maintain that there is an afterlife would, of course, be folly in the absence of evidence for the existence of a supremely perfect being who guarantees that justice prevails in the end and, hence, who brings about human survival of death. For there is no doubt that only an omnipotent being (or, anyway, a being who is powerful enough to violate some of the laws of nature) could bring about survival of earthly death. But Chapter 2 provides us with a reason for believing that a supremely perfect being in fact exists, and the concept of such a being is tightly linked to the concept of omnipotence.

10.6 At the end of the Roman Catholic Act of Contrition, one says that one regrets one's sins 'because I dread the loss of heaven and the pains of hell, but most of all because they offend thee, O my God, who art all good and deserving of all my love'. One who recites the latter words sincerely is said to have made a perfect Act of Contrition; and that is thought to be superior to admissions of guilt which are motivated only by dread of God's punishment. Nothing which I have asserted in this chapter is intended to deny this view of the proper relationship of sinners to God.

Appendix

The reader may well ask for a precise account of how (1) the SPIO's being for or against something, X, plus (2) X's being desire-satisfying or desire-frustrating, plus, finally, (3) the overriding importance to a person of performing or not performing X relate to (a) X's being morally good or bad and (b) the concept of morality.

The answer is that what I have called 'a non-semantic identity' holds between (1), (2) and (3) and X's being morally good or bad, in the sense that each is a non-semantically necessary condition of the moral goodness or badness of X and all three are jointly non-semantically sufficient for the moral goodness or badness of X, and that the concept of morality is simply the concept of something's being morally good or bad. (The reader is invited to refer back to 1.3 for my characterization of non-semantic identity. A *semantic* analysis of 'morally good' and 'morally bad' is also to be found in that section.)

I have said in effect that one's doing a service for money, on a given occasion, though it may well be desire-satisfying, usually does not count as doing something which is morally good. And we are now in a position to see that the reason is that, though doing so is desire-satisfying, and may be such that IOs approve of it, it is not of overriding importance to the doer of it that it be done. But not only may the desire to make money disqualify an action which achieves that goal from being morally good; it may well also be true that, say, the satisfaction of a sexual desire to be utterly humiliated (see *The Story of O*) is not morally good, and, indeed, is morally bad instead, even though the satisfaction of the envisaged desire does not result in a balance of desire-frustration over desire-satisfaction. We are now in a position to understand this: desires of the kind which are under

Appendix

discussion are either such that it is not of overriding importance that one satisfy them, or the SPIO does not approve of
their being satisfied, or (what is likely with respect to some
sexual desires) both.

Notes

PREFACE

1. J. L. Mackie, *Ethics, Inventing Right and Wrong* (New York: Penguin, 1977) p. 38.
2. Bernard Williams, *Ethics and the Limits of Philosophy* (Cambridge, Mass.: Harvard University Press, 1986).

CHAPTER 1   SOME ATTITUDE THEORIES OF MORALITY

1. A. J. Ayer, *Language, Truth and Logic* (New York: Dover, 1952) p. 104.
2. Ibid., pp. 104–5.
3. Ibid., p. 107.
4. Ibid., p. 108.
5. Similar considerations apply to the prescriptivist theory of R. M. Hare. See Hare's *Freedom and Reason* (London: Oxford University Press, 1963) and *Moral Thinking* (Oxford: Clarendon Press, 1981). I shall have more to say about Hare's theory in Chapter 10.
6. Clement Dore, 'Ethical Supernaturalism', *Sophia*, Oct 1976, pp. 21–2.
7. A Kripkean connection will, of course, do here as well as a Smart–Armstrong connection, i.e. necessary, as opposed to contingent, identities will serve, so long as the former are not what I am calling 'semantic'. (Indeed, I now think that the Kripkean approach to non-semantic identity is correct.)
8. See for example William G. Lycan, 'Moral Facts and Moral Knowledge', *Southern Journal of Philosophy*, XXIV, supplementary (1985) 80–1.
9. The reason for the qualifier 'empirical' is that, as we shall see, there is a supremely authoritative, non-empirical IO, and human IOs need not know of him in order to qualify as IOs.

10. The reason for the qualifier will become plain in the Appendix.
11. See note 10.
12. The IO theorist might be inclined to say here that *most* equally
    qualified judges would be, say, opposed to the threat of
    nuclear retaliation. But how does he know? Must a qualified
    judge be a polling-expert?

CHAPTER 2   A PROOF OF THE EXISTENCE OF GOD

1. *The Philosophical Works of Descartes*, tr. Elizabeth S. Haldane
   and G. R. T. Ross (New York: Dover, 1955) I, 181.
2. Alvin Plantinga, 'Is Theism Really a Miracle?', *Faith and
   Philosophy*, 3 (Apr 1986) 114–15.
3. I am defining '*supremely* perfect being' here and taking 'perfect'
   as primitive.
4. Anthony Kenny has pointed out that Descartes explained to a
   critic that by 'a mountain without a valley' he meant an uphill
   slope without a downhill slope. Anthony Kenny, *Descartes: A
   Study of his Philosophy* (New York: Random House, 1968)
   p. 156.
5. I am indebted to Alvin Plantinga here. See his distinction
   between predicative and impredicative singular propositions
   in *The Nature of Necessity* (Oxford: Clarendon Press, 1974)
   pp. 149–51.

CHAPTER 3   AGNOSTICISM AND THE ATHEISTIC
ARGUMENT FROM SUFFERING

1. As we shall see in 5.12, this claim needs qualification.

CHAPTER 4   A PROOF OF THE IDEAL-OBSERVER
THEORY

1. The reason for the qualifier will become plain in the Appendix.
2. See note 1.
3. It may well be, however, that at least many witch-burners

were not morally responsible for their ignorance. (The Bible says 'Thou shall not suffer a witch to live'.) Why, then, did God permit them to be ignorant? The answer is that their ignorance falls under the heading of the problem of evil, which will be discussed in the next chapter and in 4.11.

4. Clement Dore, *God, Suffering and Solipsism* (London: Macmillan; New York: St Martin's Press, 1989), chs 8 and 9.
5. I am indebted to Mylan Engel for this example.
6. Alvin Plantinga, 'Theism and Justification', *Faith and Philosophy*, 4 (Oct 1987) 423–4.
7. Alvin Plantinga, 'Positive Epistemic Status and Proper Function', in James Tomberlin (ed.), *Topics in Philosophy*, II: *Epistemology* (Northridge: California State University, 1988).

CHAPTER 5   THE PROBLEM OF MORAL EVIL

1. Plantinga, *The Nature of Necessity* pp. 164–95.
2. Ibid., pp. 186–9.
3. J. L. Mackie, *The Miracle of Theism* (New York: Oxford University Press, 1982) p. 174.
4. Antony Flew and Alasdair MacIntyre (eds), *New Essays in Philosophical Theology* (London: SCM Press, 1955) pp. 149–51.
5. Mackie, *The Miracle of Theism*, pp. 169–70, 172.
6. Plantinga, *The Nature of Necessity*, pp. 167–80, pp. 187–8.
7. Robert Merrihew Adams, 'Middle Knowledge and the Problem of Evil', *American Philosophical Quarterly*, 14 (Apr 1977).
8. Ibid., p. 109.
9. Plantinga, *The Nature of Necessity*, p. 192.
10. Clement Dore, *Theism* (Dordrecht: D. Reidel, 1984) p. 60, and *God, Suffering and Solipsism*, ch. 9.

CHAPTER 6   DESIRE-UTILITARIANISM

1. It may be thought that standard utilitarianism also entails that the killing of *adults* would be warranted in these circum-

stances. But that is clearly not true. For the killing of adults might give rise to fear on the part of other adults that they, too, will be killed, in similar circumstances. And people desire not to be thus afraid.

2. '. . . it is difficult to see any sound moral justification for the view that distance . . . makes a crucial difference to our obligations' – Peter Singer, *Practical Ethics* (Cambridge: Cambridge University Press, 1979) p. 170. See also pp. 168–9.

CHAPTER 7 INFANTICIDE, I

1. Michael Tooley, 'A Defense of Abortion and Infanticide', in Joel Feinberg (ed.), *The Problem of Abortion*, 1st edn (Belmont, Calif.: Wadsworth, 1973) pp. 51–91, and 'A Defense of Abortion and Infanticide', in Feinberg, *The Problem of Abortion*, 2nd edn (1984) pp. 120–34. I shall consider only the first of these two articles, since I think that the arguments in the first are more persuasive than those in the second.

2. Tooley, in Feinberg, *The Problem of Abortion*, 1st edn, pp. 86–8. I have replaced the kittens in Tooley's thought-experiment with (less intuition-muddying) retarded infants. In Tooley's example, the injected kitten will develop a complex human consciousness if not interfered with. In the altered example, the severely retarded infant will desire continued life in the near future if not interfered with. There is no reason why Tooley should object to these changes.

3. Judith Jarvis Thompson, 'A Defense of Abortion', in Feinberg, *The Problem of Abortion*, 2nd edn, p. 174.

4. Ibid., p. 180.

5. Ibid., p. 175.

6. Ibid., p. 184.

7. Ibid., p.186.

CHAPTER 8 INFANTICIDE, II

1. Joel Feinberg, 'Potentiality, Development and Rights', in Feinberg, *The Problem of Abortion*, 2nd edn, p. 115.

2. John T. Noonan, 'An Almost Absolute Value in Human History', in Feinberg, *The Problem of Abortion*, 1st edn, pp. 15ff.
3. Peter Unger, 'I Do Not Exist', in G. F. MacDonald (ed.), *Perception and Identity* (Ithaca, NY: Cornell University Press, 1979) p. 241.
4. Ibid., pp. 237–9.

CHAPTER 9   THE DOCTRINE OF DOUBLE EFFECT

1. I have taken the example from Jonathan Bennett's 'Morality and Consequence', in James P. Sterba (ed.), *The Ethics of War and Nuclear Deterrence* (Belmont, Calif.: Wadsworth, 1985) pp. 23–4. Bennett comes to the conclusion that there is no morally relevant difference between them. I come to the opposite conclusion.
2. Philippa Foot, *Virtue and Vices and Other Essays in Moral Philosophy* (Berkeley Calif.: University of California Press, 1978) pp. 21–2.
3. Gilbert Harman, *The Nature of Morality* (New York: Oxford University Press, 1977) p. 156.
4. James Montmarquet, 'On Doing Good: The Right and the Wrong Way', *Journal of Philosophy*, 79 (Aug 1982) 440.
5. Foot, *Virtues and Vices*, p. 23.
6. Montmarquet, in *Journal of Philosophy*, 79, pp. 446–7.
7. Ibid., p. 452.
8. Ibid., p. 453.
9. Ibid., pp. 446, 453.
10. Ibid., pp. 446–7.
11. Foot, *Virtues and Vices*, p. 29.
12. US Catholic Bishops, 'On the Use of Nuclear Weapons and Nuclear Deterrence', in Sterba, *The Ethics of War*, pp. 139–46. The bishops evidently think that the United States can successfully pose a nuclear threat to the Soviet Union without intending to carry it out. Here, I think, they are mistaken. Sterba (ibid., pp. 163–6) argues in effect that the United States should retain a nuclear force but make it clear that it does not intend to use it under present circumstances. He

thinks that this is a morally welcome alternative to actually threatening nuclear destruction. But I cannot see that it is. For, if the Soviets were to carry out a first strike on the United States, then the circumstances in which it would allegedly be immoral for the United States to threaten nuclear destruction would *eo ipso* have been abolished. If I'm right here, then there *is* no way of failing to threaten nuclear destruction short of actually planning not to carry out the threat.

13. I think that it will not be IO-intuition-violating if we let *C* apply to the case in which, since the antecedents of the envisaged counterfactuals ae necessarily false, they also entail that it is *false* that God would have performed the contemplated actions, and with a similar motive.

14. Judith Jarvis Thompson, 'Rights and Deaths', in Cohen, Nagel and Scanlon (eds), *The Rights and Wrongs of Abortion* (Princeton, NJ: Princeton University Press, 1974) p. 119.

CHAPTER 10   MORAL AND NON-MORAL VALUE

1. The reason for the qualifier will become clear in the Appendix.
2. Hare, *Freedom and Reason*, pp. 168–9.
3. Ibid. This appears to be his position on pp. 176–7.
4. Hare, *Moral Thinking*, p. 57.
5. Ibid., pp. 60–1.

Index